D1372475

COMPLETE GUIDE TO FISHING

Ice Fishing

HANS NORDIN

COMPLETE GUIDE TO FISHING

Ice Fishing

MASON CREST PUBLISHERS, INC.

COMPLETE GUIDE TO FISHING – **Ice Fishing**
has been originated, produced and designed by
AB Nordbok, Gothenburg, Sweden.

Publisher
Gunnar Stenmar

Editorial chief
Anders Walberg

Design, setting & photowork:
Reproman AB, Gothenburg, Sweden

Translator:
Jon van Leuven

Nordbok would like to express sincere thanks to all
persons and companies who have contributed in
different ways to the production of this book.

World copyright © 2002
Nordbok International,
P.O.Box 7095,
SE-402 32 Gothenburg, Sweden.

Published in the United States by
Mason Crest Publishers, Inc.
370 Reed Road, Broomall, PA 19008
(866) MCP-BOOK (toll free)
www.masoncrest.com

First printing
1 2 3 4 5 6 7 8 9 10
Library of Congress Cataloging-in-Publication Data on file at
the Library of Congress

ISBN 1-59084-497-1

Printed and bound in the Hashemite Kingdom of Jordan

Contents

Preface

Discoveries are not made only at the frontiers of science. Most of them are probably more like personal revelations in an ordinary person's everyday life and activities. Such a revelation came to me when I began ice-angling some years ago. Admittedly, I had already tried other kinds of fishing on ice and enjoyed them very much. But it was first with ice-angling that I realized what dormant potential of qualified and abundant sportfishing awaits us beneath the winter ice's roof. Today I have ice-angling to thank for a great deal. This revelation led me to reconquer winter itself, which was lost for me at the end of childhood. The discovery that ice-angling belongs so closely to wintertime has, therefore, not only left tracks in my fishing soul, but also given a better balance to my life as a whole.

Due to the advent of cell phones and computers during the past decade, linking up and communicating nonstop are regarded as "in", while silence and solitude are "out". Still, one may wonder what is happening to our need for relaxation, as well as our occasional need to find ourselves decoupled in "dead time".

The silence, calm and seclusion on the winter ice offer me – in addition to the pleasure of fishing and liberation – an opportunity to reflex and pause, sort out and collect myself, at least during the intervals between bites. I prefer to stay a little behind the float in the radio shadow even on the ice, as a plain protest in any case. Perhaps it is among sportfishermen, anglers and other wilderness-lovers that the "rebels" of our age can be found.

As I pass this book along now, I do so in full awareness that a great deal more remains to be investigated about fish behaviour and the possibilities for ice-angling. If in these pages I nevertheless sound at times certain or categorical in my advice and conclusions, I hope that the reader will excuse me when experiences occur that expose the shortcomings of my own presentation. Ideally this book will have helped to inspire discoveries, experiences, new skills – and reduced the time between bites – if such be the point of this wonderfully serious game.

Hans Nordin

Fishing equipment

The title of this book, "Modern ice-angling", was chosen in order to emphasize angling, but also to show that the book does not deal with traditional ice-fishing, although the latter's gear can still be of excellent help to a winter fisherman who wants to try a new way of using the gear. There is probably no "sportfishing-like" method older than angling. Oddly enough, angling has tended to be popular almost solely during the summer season, whereas ice-fishing has contented itself with traditional approaches.

In what follows, I will describe how successful angling from the ice can be done for our most common and sought-after predatory fish. Basically, two methods of angling are to be discussed. The difference between them is really just a matter of which equipment you choose to use – modern rods with reels, or traditional types of ice-fishing gear that are converted to angle with. Personally I get most enjoyment from older gear which has been adjusted and re-rigged for angling as described in this book. But my preference may be individual, and the reason is perhaps that I belong to a previous generation. From the start of my path as a winter fisherman, I have grown up and become familiar with the use of ice-fishing gear.

Traditional fishing with such gear has played, and still plays, a major role as a general pastime. There is something splendid about this fishing. And historically, it has often been connected with social hobnobbing – which abruptly, but only temporarily, is interrupted when a champagne cork has been fired off and signalled a bite.

Exactly how this way of fishing in the winter developed is a good question.

Ice-fishing gear: old equipment with great potential. When properly designed it serves for all kinds of predatory fish.

The angling rod is a wooden stick about 25 cm long, usually bevelled at the lower end to be stuck firmly in the ice. Fixed on the rod is a line reel that holds 15-20 metres of thick line. At the top is mounted the "rocker", consisting of a long thin leaf-spring and a small red signal-cork or the like. The rod is also commonly provided with an acoustic signalling device (popping cork) which is fired off at the bite.

The history of ice-angling

Towards the end of the eighteenth century, an English ship and crew were trapped by the ice for a whole winter. To pass the time and, no doubt, to vary their supply of food, these Englishmen began to fish from the ice. A small booklet entitled "The new winter angling" was published in 1787. This eight-page work is both a detailed guide on ice-angling and a reportage on what happened during the winter in question.

The traditional ice-fishing rod deserves all respect. It has survived and acquired new passionate enthusiasts with a march of victory that has lasted for just over 200 years. The fact that the equipment has not changed much since then is naturally a confirmation. The hook has become more vertical and sharply angled by comparison with the more C-shaped hooks (with a straight lower part) that were forged at first. Other additions have been a more modern (but equally thick) fishing line, and a popping cork. On the whole, however, this fine and simple rod is still intact in its historical form.

Opposite page:
When a pike has taken the bait, it immediately begins to swim away with the line. The fisherman notes which side the pike heads for, then takes his stand at the opposite side of the ice hole. Thereafter, he makes a well-timed strike.

Left:
Ice-fishing rod with a pike in the foreground. In the background a fisherman comes running over the ice towards the rod, which has just "sprung". A bite again!

Below:
Angling hooks, one with a roach and one without. The special angling hook is very large, and bent so that a biting fish – a pike – cannot swallow the bait but only holds it in the mouth.

In all its simplicity, the classic kind of ice-fishing rod is a virtually perfect set of equipment. And the magic that the rod conveys when the rocker stands knocking, at the same time as the line reel rotates, is hard to beat in the way of bite excitement.

Another very special feature of ice-angling is that every biting fish is hooked and played by hand. This leads quickly to a serious addiction with a high resistance to abstinence among the practitioners.

Now and then in the fishing press, innovations are presented that supposedly improve ice-angling in one way or another. But I myself have yet to see any innovation that appears more suitable to fish with, if it concerns ice-angling with a traditional angling hook. Neither has any of these innovations satisfactorily solved the problem of the limitations of ice-fishing gear when it comes to fishing for other species than pike.

Using the traditional gear

The fishing procedure is that the large hook is threaded under the skin of a fish from behind, until the hook tip reaches the bait's nape. Then the bait is sunk down to 30 cm above the bottom. A loop is tied on the line and hung over the somewhat upward-bent leaf-feather's outermost part, so that the baitfish hangs at the intended fishing depth. At a bite, the line loop comes free from the leaf-feather, which flips up and waves back and forth. If the rod is provided with a popping cork and a release mechanism for it, the cork will be fired off when the feather flips up. It is almost impossible to miss a bite, and this can be important for the fishing results. Since the biting fish cannot swallow the bait, it will soon spit out the bait unless the angler hooks it first.

But a pike should not be hooked too soon.

After a short time, the pike stops to try and turn the baitfish so that it can be swallowed. Then the angling hook will reach the right position in the pike's mouth. When the pike begins to swim again, it is time for the fisherman to make a strike.

Finally the pike is hauled towards the hole with smooth pulls, and is swept up onto the ice through the big angling hole. In traditional ice-fishing, it is important that the retrieval be done at an even, uninterrupted pace, so that there is never a slack line or a pause. This is because the large hook can easily come loose from the fish's jaw. The hole in the ice where the angling is done must be big in order to prevent the hook itself from catching in the ice edge, when the pike is swept up onto the ice in a single movement.

Despite the effectiveness of ice-fishing gear when pike fishing on winter ice, it must be concluded that such equipment, in traditional form, has limited range for angling in general. And this is a limitation that actually applies not only to other species such as salmonoids, pikeperch and perch. Even pike can sometimes be very difficult to succeed with, when the fishing is done with an ice-fishing hook!

The last statement may sound heretical to a devoted traditionalist, but is none the less true for that. Besides, who would think of fishing for pike with an angling hook during the ice-free part of the year? Possibly those who fish with a dead, slimy baitfish and want it to hang about right in the water. Yet as Mikael ("Micko") Bergström – a colourful inspector, fishing guide, and fish conservation officer for certain put-and-take waters in Sweden – so strikingly expressed it once, when pike were to be taken away for reasons of conservation: "What pike would attack a roach that is standing stiff as a cane, leaning forward like a ski jumper? Not a pike with its wits about it, anyhow." This utterance followed an afternoon which had become ever slower for fishing, and when the present author, having begun the day by catching five pike with the method in question, finally hooked a further thirteen pike on converted ice-fishing gear, while the fishing with traditional gear at the same place and time yielded only a single contact.

Even the most skilful and devoted ice-fishing enthusiast will fairly soon bow to that fact, once allowed to test and compare catch results with the techniques advised in this book.

On a purchased ice-fishing rod, the original line can be left in place. With some turns of tape around the line to encapsulate it, the reel becomes a spool with a thick line drum. Above this, it is easy to tie and wind on a new fishing line of plain nylon.

Converted ice-angling gear

In its traditional form, an ice-fishing rod works really well only for pike fishing. But not even there, in my opinion, is it perfect. The thick line and the typical angling hook make the whole set-up clumsy and crude. This lack of refinement limits its usability. However, the traditional rod can easily be altered in certain respects to become a qualified ice-angling assemblage that serves for all predatory fish – and on all occasions. It will then also function better for catching pike.

Change the line and make the reel drum thicker

The "barbed wire" that sits on the ice-fishing rod when you buy it must be removed, together with the angling hook. Instead, about 50 metres of thinner and lighter line are wound on: an ordinary 0.35-mm nylon line. Next, the tackle is rigged in the usual angling manner, with a small sinker farthest up above a fairly long leader and, farthest down on the line, a small treble hook or a single hook.

The budgie tinkler or eel bell – a refined bite indicator

Bites that occur in ice-angling can be both spectacular and dramatic. And we human beings are creatures of habit. Not surprisingly, then, even the bang from a fired-off cork may become an integral part of the central experience in every theatre of sportfishing – the bite.

Not every fisherman, though, is thrilled by a cork going off. In my case, moreover, I have found that fishing with a cork indicator has a passivizing influence on me as a fisherman. By contrast, fishing without one makes me more active, alert, present and observant. I would also claim that my catches have thereby increased considerably.

For if you rely on your own senses, you turn into an active scout on the ice. Your eyes move constantly back and forth between the fishing rods. If you also equip your rods with so-called budgie or eel bells, you become a listening fisherman as well. What you listen for is the unobtrusive tinkle which announces that a predatory fish was just there and clapped its jaws around a bait somewhere. "Tinkle," it says. And at that signal, your eyes scout even more intensively to locate the rod that gave the sound. Sometimes it can take up to half a minute's scanning before a rocker is slowly pulled down and reveals the hidden hunter's position.

When a fish takes the bait in this way, the outcome may instead be an interrupted bite. The fish keeps pulling and the signal feather is gradually bent ever deeper – until the fish may spit out the bait because, in the end, it cannot complete the effort. This emphasizes the point of staying alert and also listening for the "tinkle". Before the fish possibly spits, and thus stops biting, an alert fisherman glides forward to the spot and helps it out with an "emergency felling". The line loop is loosened from the rocker, reducing the resistance that disturbs the fish. As a result, a hesitant and sluggish fish may carry out its original impulse rather than abandoning the bait.

Another advantage of the "tinkle" that warns about bites is that the fisherman often makes it to the spot in good time and can check that things are going as they should – that the line is not tangling in any way, the reel does not become sluggish with ice formation, or the like.

If a winter fisherman prefers hand equipment for angling from the ice, the most convenient choice is to use some form of casting gear. A good casting set-up will not only improve the fisherman's possibilities of bringing home the catch once it sits on the hook. Fishing with a casting rod also avoids the complications that can arise when you play by hand with a line lying loose on the ice. Moreover, with approved hand equipment, a caught fish will be approved by the sportfishing registry of big fish, if your quarry turns out to be of that calibre.

Short rods with baitcasting reels

The equipment can consist of an ordinary rod and reel for spinning and baitcasting. Most important is that the reel works well. Ideally it should also be possible to release the reel without letting line blow loose from the spool and wrapping around chunks of ice or the like – or to have a finely adjustable drag brake that can be set loosely enough for a biting fish to pull out line without feeling resistance. Most types of multiplier reel are excellent at this. A spinning reel is often worse for these purposes, but functions on "clean" ice under windless conditions. It is best to attach the line to a release when the reel bail is open. In well-assorted sportfishing shops, ready-made line releases can be bought for mounting on baitcasting rods.

When ice-angling, I have tried everything from a short 5-foot boat rod to a 2-foot ice-fishing rod. But also complete baitcasting rods or divided ones with the upper section left at home have been used. The latter arrangement has the drawback of a dull feeling when playing the fish. It resembles fishing with a stiff boat rod. Fishing with too long a rod also has disadvantages – the fisherman stays too far from the hole where the fish is being played.

Since playing the fish is most enjoyable on a rod that is not too stiff, it can be rewarding to search for suitable rods. Here follow some tips for winter angling: a special rod for qualified pike angling from the ice, and a more all-round rod that works superbly for less enormous fish – pikeperch, rainbow trout, large perch, and pike of normal size.

Manufacturers and retailers of equipment are becoming aware that ever more sportfishermen have discovered the great pleasure and potential of ice-angling. Hence, I hope and believe that within the near future we shall see a wider range of rods on the market which are adapted to winter angling in particular. With luck we can look forward to the development of more equipment that is really good.

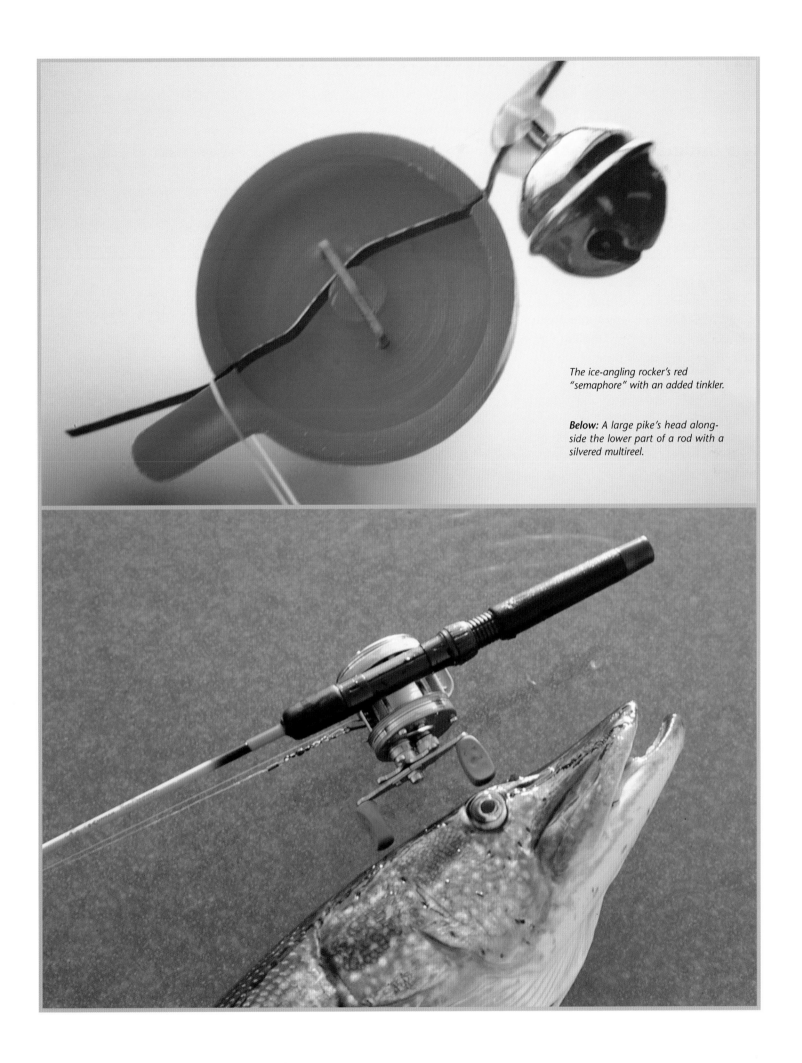

The ice-angling rocker's red "semaphore" with an added tinkler.

Below: A large pike's head alongside the lower part of a rod with a silvered multireel.

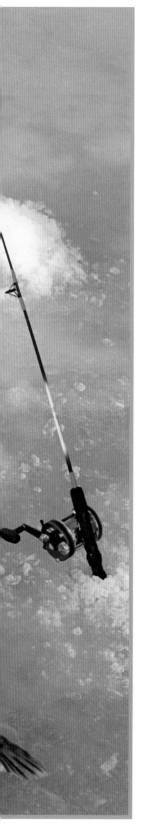

Far left:
White-toned rod with long handle, standing on ice with a pike lying: Abu Garcia offers a soft boat road
(Royal Commodore 4') which has become popular in ice-angling for pike. The rod has a spine for heavy pike fishing.

Left:
Blue-toned, somewhat shorter rod with a short handle, with a pike lying on the ice: KingFisher sells a shorter rod
(Cannon Herring 3'), an excellent all-round rod for big pike, rainbow trout, normal pike and so on. It is really fun
to play the fish with. On the strike, the rod acquires more "spine" if the fisherman takes a couple of steps backward!

Above:
Angling with a float works in the winter too. But if there is much snow on the ice, it can be hard to see when a float
dives – especially if several rods are spread over a large area. Unfortunately, predatory fish in winter are often
extra-sensitive to the resistance a float gives at bites. A float functions best for pike angling.

Left:
Together with a line release, a colourful plastic rosette can serve well. If the rosette is tied on the line up towards the rod tip, it is nice to watch how the rosette begins its turn down towards the hole at the bite, and finally disappears.

Below:
On a fairly stiff rod, a small bent plastic tube of suitable diameter is glued or taped, for the angling rocker or leaf-feather to be inserted in.

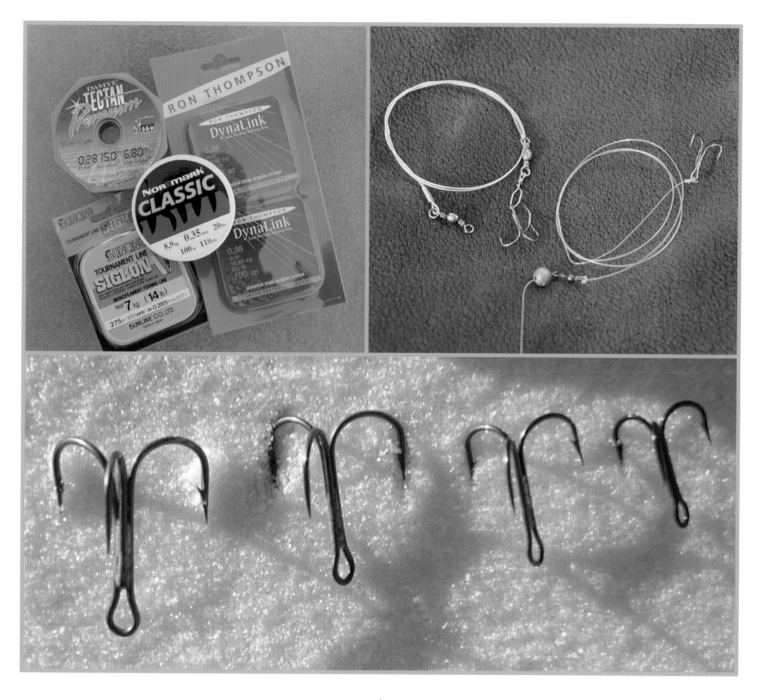

Top left:
A good thin pike line should take about 7-12 kg if you also expect big ones. Thus, a nylon line should be 0.35-0.40 mm thick. A corresponding line for perch and pikeperch is 0.30-0.35 mm. For all-round ice-angling, 0.35 mm is therefore the best choice.

Above:
For pike as well as perch and pikeperch, fairly small treble hooks can be used to advantage. A treble hook of size No. 6 works excellently on all three species. Hook sizes No. 4 and No. 2 may serve for pure pike fishing, especially with large baitfish. When pike fishing with a hook tackle that has two hooks, Nos. 6-8 are appropriate.

Top right:
For pike, only one leader works – a steel wire. This is the only kind that lasts! For other ice-angling an all-round leader made of 0.50-mm nylon line is recommended. This leader works superbly for both perch and pikeperch as well as salmonoids. A leader length of 50-70 cm increases the live bait's mobility. A long leader also protects against line breakage in case a big pike has time to swallow. Another reason for using a long leader is that, not seldom, a pike begins to rotate and rolls itself up in the line. A longer leader protects, at least, against one turn of the rolling if the pike then gets the leader between its teeth.

Rods and other equipment

Tackle

The bait's mobility – its capacity and endurance for swimming round in wide circles – depends on the resistance and weights it is anchored with. The baits that move best and over the largest areas will attract the most predatory fish to bite: this is the main rule. Hence, you have to "think light" when it comes to tackle. A pitiful bait that almost absurdly wobbles under the burden of an all too heavy sinker or big hook, or too stiff and heavy a leader, does not excite a hesitant fish to any heroic deeds.

One should be very watchful of the damage a nylon leader easily causes. With small scratches and "shuck" on the nylon leader, it is time either to cut the leader a bit, or to simply tie a new one. Otherwise the next pike, or even a pikeperch, will bite off the line when its teeth catch in the leader's scratches.

Transport on the ice

An enthusiastic ice-angler soon needs to arrange transport across the ice. It will not do for long to drag all your fishing accessories, rods, angling rod, bait-buckets, sleeping bag, drill brace, ice scoop and ice stick, etc. in a disorganized way.

Sledge

An ample sledge is an adequate temporary solution – especially if it will not be pulled through forests or over rough terrain. Under such conditions it keeps tipping over and spilling out the equipment.

Top right:
Moraspiralen and Viking are two of the ice drills with greatest value for money on the market. Competition fishermen's favourite is Rantanen, which is very easy to drill with. The 150-mm drill can deal with pikeperch of 6.0-6.5 kg, perch over 1.5 kg, and pike of around 10 kg. For larger fish, a drill diameter of 175-205 mm is recommended.

Bottom right:
An ice scoop is for repeated clearing of ice from the borehole that is used for fishing – and for picking up bait from the cold water in a bait-bucket.

An ice pick leaning against a big blue bait-basket:
This tool is for making large holes in the ice. Roach huts and bait-baskets are also used in traditional ice-angling. Caution: an ice pick is easy to lose through the ice, so anchor it with a safety loop fastened firmly around your wrist!

A bait-bucket with live bait must have a good cover that sits tightly, so that the water will not slosh out. On really cold days, a non-insulated bait-bucket is exposed to rapid freezing inside, which numbs the live baitfish. An ordinary refrigerator solves these problems.

A collapsible scooter – of the Flexsparken type shown here – is easy to transport by car. The transport sled, loaded with all its equipment, can easily be lashed onto the scooter's seat. Then you need only kick away on safe ice to new and distant fishing waters.

Here is a simple and very functional transport sled that you can make yourself. It is steady and quite roomy. You need a 50-litre plastic crate, and a pair of worn-out slalom skis (with plastic bottoms!) cut to adequate length as in the picture. Screw the crate on, and attach an old plastic seat-mat between the ski tips. The pull-rope is run through the seat-mat's handle, and helps to hold the bait-bucket in place.

Safety equipment and clothing

There are places and ice conditions in which one should always take extra care – especially during the beginning and end of the ice-fishing season, when the ice tends to be unusually thin and weak, with a greater risk of falling through.

Risk areas on the ice

A fall through the ice can be due to several factors: poor knowledge of ice, naïve optimism, too much socializing, or a few seconds' inattention.

Watch out for areas with flowing waters – inlets and outlets. Also exposed to currents that can weaken the ice are narrow straits and promontories. Because of currents, too, you should be careful about underwater shallows. The same is true of heat-radiating obstacles in the ice – piers, bridge pillars, protruding vegetation and so on. In addition, one has to exercise caution near open channels and fairways – and when in areas of unknown ice. Among the most treacherous phenomena on winter ice are so-called wind wells, areas where the ice has not frozen properly due to wind and water currents.

Some common areas with risky ice are illustrated here: promontories, currents, straits, vegetation, piers, open channels.

ICE STICK This accessory is very good for feeling your way on insecure ice. An ice pick can also serve as a feeler. The ideal ice pick is both easy to carry and heavy enough to test the ice's thickness with. But a ski pole is insufficient.

ICE PRODS There is no cheaper or better life insurance than this! With ice prods, you can get yourself out of the water even when the ice is hard, slippery and smooth. The prods should be fastened around your neck, high under the jaw, so that they can easily be got hold of.

LIFELINE This can rescue other people who have fallen through the ice. The line should be buoyant and strong, and able to run without tangling. It should also be thick enough so that even frozen fingers are able to grip it.

WHISTLE This is useful for attracting attention if you yourself get in trouble, but also when you want to warn others about dangerous ice you encounter.

MOBILE TELEPHONE In a serious situation, every minute can be vital. On ice, your cell phone should be kept easily available in a well-closed watertight plastic bag.

BUOYANCY OVERALLS The virtues of buoyancy overalls as both clothing and life insurance can hardly be overestimated. This suit gives you the properties of three in one – warm overalls, a rainsuit, and a life-jacket.

Above: *Ice prods, whistle, lifeline and cell phone: some of the winter fisherman's most important items of equipment.*

Left: *A fisherman on his knees wearing buoyancy overalls, and ice prods where they should be – under the jaw.*

The ice changes – watch out!

Clear ice

No ice is stronger and tougher than this particular kind. As clear ice grows, it becomes ever stronger and forms the winter ice's foundation.

As long as the ice is firm and hard, the following thicknesses are a guide to how much weight the ice can support:

4   cm of ice support 80 kg, an adult person.

10 cm of ice support 600 kg, about 6 persons with gear.

15 cm of ice support 1200 kg, equivalent to a small car.

25 cm of ice support 3600 kg, equivalent to a tractor.

However, this does not mean just tramping out on the ice when it is 4 cm thick. Besides, the ice thickness varies too much. And the fisherman's total weight – with equipment, sled, bait-buckets, sleeping bag etc. – can be well over 100 kg. Preferably wait for a few cold, snow-free nights more!

Slush-ice or double ice

Sometimes we encounter ice that is completely grey and granular. It is formed by snow and water that have frozen together. This so-called slush-ice (or double ice) can be very tricky, especially if it arises at an early stage in winter.

The phenomenon of slush-ice may also occur at any time during the winter – when the ice base has for some reason acquired a substantial cover of water and, at the same time, a blanket of snow lies on top. The snow mixes with the water and freezes, but not enough. Between the two ice layers, water is still present and can make a walk on the top difficult if you constantly break through the slush-ice.

Open channels

The formation of open channels should also be kept in mind during winter. These occur because of tension in the ice, and are most common in wide waters or along coastal archipelagos. There are three types of channels that arise due to big cracks in the ice.

In a so-called sink-channel, the ice edges are instead pressed towards each other and downward. Such ice pits can be surprisingly deep.

Top right: *The tip of an ice pick reflected in blue ice: The first ice that is laid down on a cold, windless winter night is called clear (blue) ice. It looks dark but is actually quite clear and transparent.*

Bottom right: *Grey, granular ice with some reed stalks: There is a risk that the hard surface we are eager to walk on consists of an illusory shell, looking stronger than it is. Even open wind-wells, in the middle of a lake that has clear ice elsewhere, can be covered by such a treacherous crust of grey, granular ice.*

The third type of open channel is known as a rise channel. It occurs when the ice edges are pressed towards each other and upward. The ice piles up visibly and may be unreliable. The same is true of areas with pack ice that occur when ice floes are pressed together in layer upon layer by the wind.

The most treacherous type of open channel occurs when ice masses are separated by a crack and drift apart (as is also common in fairways). Then large areas of open water are exposed and create a risk when the new ice is covered by snow.

Treacherous spring ice

The ice changes with varying weather and increasing age. Popular fishing places can suddenly become perilous to visit. During the winter-to-spring transition, one should put trust in ice that has borne up all winter under rigorous testing. The sun and the ever warmer days will be taking a toll of the ice. One should avoid passing through reeds or approaching large buoys, which are also heat-radiating and weaken the ice.

The imposing grey ice is soon turned into an ever more hollow and sometimes dark "stave ice". While the increasingly warm spring water begins to circulate and wear away the ice from below, sunshine and rain are melting it from above.

The stave ice consists of ice rods with pipe-like holes between them, where the melt-water runs down. After a cold night, the ice rods freeze and the layer is 40 cm thick, looking as strong as any. Yet only some hours later, when the sun has been shining, it can be dangerous to step on. A couple of days after that, it may have vanished and left the water completely open.

Reminders about clothes and weather

The key rule for experienced outdoorsmen is to keep the body dry during physical exertion, so that one can sit for long later as well. This is often achieved today by using physiological underwear next to the body. Such underwear provides ventilation and releases moisture, allowing the skin to remain dry. But since the sweat must go somewhere, it is recommended to wear a layer of moisture-absorbing cotton garments over physiological underwear.

Take account of the wind's cooling effect

It is often extremely cold out on the open, exposed ice. And the harder the wind blows, the colder it becomes. The wind's cooling factor is definitely something to be remembered when heading out on lakes. As some examples of what can be expected, a land-based temperature of 0°C (32°F) changes with the wind strength as follows:

   5 m/sec: -8°C (+18°F)
   10 m/sec: -15°C (+5°F)
   15m/sec: -18°C (-0°F)

   If the land-based temperature with no wind is a respectable -10°C (+14°F), the cold changes with the wind strength thus:

   5 m/sec: -21°C (-6°F)
   10 m/sec: -30°C (-22°F)
   15 m/sec: -34°C (-29°F)

Footwear

What we have on our feet is as important as anything else when it comes to keeping the cold out and the fishing pleasure present. In general, the point is to cover the feet warmly and airily, that is, not too tightly. At least one number bigger than the normal size of footwear will leave room for thick extra socks without any squeezing.

Headgear

A head without a cap is like a chimney without a lid – all the heat escapes. Nothing more need be said.

   Or possibly also that a windproof fur cap with ear-flaps can be worth its weight in gold when a freezing wind is blowing. Otherwise a knitted wool cap is fine (and wool warms even when wet!).

Two of the best winter choices – Tretorn (ATLE) and Nokia(TURA) – boots that are warm, watertight, and nice to walk in. These specially lined boots can also have studded soles.

Northern pike
(Esox Lucius)

Seldom does one see an animal that so fully matches its own reputation in purely physical terms. Not by coincidence is it known as the wolf or crocodile of lakes, since its hunting tactics are most reminiscent of those large predators' ways. It sometimes sneaks up on its prey, or sometimes places itself in ambush hiding among the shadows of floating wood and plants. The lightning-quick attack usually comes as a total surprise, and once it has snapped its wide jaws shut over the prey's body with their 700-odd needle-sharp, backward-slanting teeth, the chances are very small of getting away.

After sixty million years of adaptation and evolution, this extremely successful hunter is now widespread in fresh and brackish waters – except for high mountain regions. Unlike perch and pikeperch, the pike is almost a cold-water fish, and it flourishes wonderfully in the cool northern climate.

Pike are loners. The reason why we sportfishermen nevertheless occasionally find many pikes loitering or hunting in the same place does not mean that pike enjoy collective activities in any kind, but has quite different causes. Apart from the spring spawning, which brings large quantities of fish together in the same areas and is due to their biological clock, there are sometimes remarkable concentrations of pike in small areas as a result of external conditions – strong wind, favourable water temperature, abundance of prey, or especially good access to camouflage. At such times, the pike tolerate company and mind their own business. But the smallest ones flee the neighbourhood as larger pike arrive. They do so for plain self-preservation, to avoid the serious risk of ending as cannibal food.

The pike's reputation as a leading predator is well-founded. An adult pike is a great fish-eater and often cannibalistic. Studies of inland pike, however, show that its main prey in most cases are roaches. Whether this is because it has a special taste for roaches, or can be explained by the good supply of that prey, is unclear since the pike is a pretty all-round eater. Field-mice, frogs, ducklings and even insects are on its menu, and can make pike fat where nothing else is available.

The pike follows a definite annual rhythm in its move-

Pike at an ice hole.

ments. After spring spawning and the early summer hunting on fish-rich shallows or in moderately deep bays, pike spend the high summer in deeper and cooler bays, preferably parking at sunken rocks and small isles in free water. From these depths, it makes only brief visits up to the shallow waters during cold, rainy periods and when hunting especially at evening or in early morning.

Once the autumn cools down the water masses to more comfortable temperatures, pike go back into shallower habitats near shore. September is therefore a good time for pike fishermen. The really big specimens reach the fishing arena later in autumn when the leaves start to fall. But the late autumn's turbulent weather system in October and November, with fast-shifting winds and temperatures, make one's pike fishing rather like a roller-coaster, as the pike react to these chaotic conditions. One day we find them in shallow waters, the next in deeper ones – one day in the lee, the next to windward, and so on, if we find them at all.

At the same time as the pike move toward shallower water to find calm surroundings and better temperatures during late autumn, their preyfish move out toward deeper and warmer water. For the surface water then becomes cooled more rapidly. The pike thus slip out to deeper water when hunting, and then return to the calmer shallows to digest their food – just the opposite of their behaviour in summer. It is these constantly changing movements, solely due to the search for food or to quick changes in weather, that often give pike fishing at such times an "all or nothing" character.

Just before the water ices up, it is coldest, and even the pike go out to find the warmest pockets of deep water. They now live in a freezing world where most things are in slow motion. But it does not take long before the ice spreads like an insulating, stabilizing cover, decreasing the heat loss from the water. Once the first ice is laid down, therefore, the pike seek protection under this roof, which provides both shadows and a steadier environment.

Since the insulating ice cover now gives the earth's heat a chance to slowly warm up the ice-cold water from below, the pike will soon revive and become their old selves again, full of appetite and ferocious to smaller fish. The pike's tolerance of cold enables it to become active before the small fish, which it can thus easily catch.

The pike's activity under the ice

Pike can be fished with great success from the ice throughout the winter. It is definitely worth trying your luck also during midwinter, even though many winter pike-fishermen prefer the simpler fishing that is done on groundwater ice near shore at the beginning and end of winter.

In high winter, when the pike are readily found on deep bottoms as well, there is some natural decline in the activity of most water-residents. This is usually said to be caused by the weaker light, due to the ever thicker ice and the snow on it. The reduction in light stops the activity among insects and other small creatures, which in turn reduces the activity of small fish that live on them. As a result, the lower end of the food chain is weakened and, farther up the chain, pike increasingly lose their interest in the surroundings and become less active too.

Personally, I do not attach much significance to these theories about the negative impact of light reduction for pike activity. In any case, they do not strike me as so important that my own desire to fish suffers. The simple reason is that pike fishing is frequently best(!) during dark and cloudy days even during high winter – and not seldom, it is worst during clear sunny days, even when there is plenty of snow on the ice. Thus, as a hunter, the pike seems highly faithful to its usual nature even in wintertime. It often hunts most intensively in the dim light of morning or dusk, even when the season is

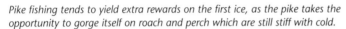

Pike fishing tends to yield extra rewards on the first ice, as the pike takes the opportunity to gorge itself on roach and perch which are still stiff with cold.

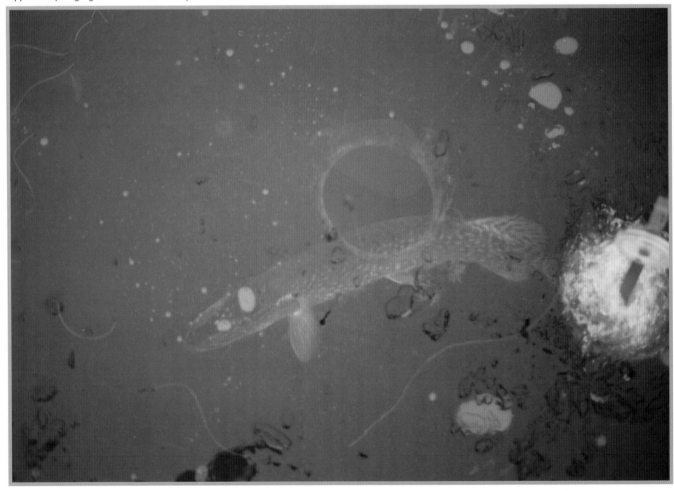

In the foreground, pike lying on ice, and two fishermen baiting their hooks again: Pike often have distinctive biting periods when there can be intensive work for fishermen who are prepared.

high winter and the ice is both thick and snow-covered! The fact is that pike are very fishable all during winter.

Moreover, winters are seldom either "normal" or static. The weather changes at intervals and, with it, so does the pike's activity and urge to bite. The same is true during high winter. And however sluggish the pike is, the weather conditions are rarely so unsuitable that there is reason to delay a planned fishing trip. Even a motionless, passive pike awakens and becomes curious when you begin to drill and pound on the ice.

The key to success when pike are rather inactive is a searching approach to the fishing!

Fishermen who drill the most holes and do not hesitate to change their locations will succeed best. But of course there are exceptional days and periods when the sport can slow down – this is nothing unique to winter. During the rest of the year as well, pike alternate highly active times with "leisurely" ones.

The transitions between the pike's very active and inactive intervals can sometimes be quite sudden. In midwinter, the fishing is often best at the junctures between different turns of the weather. Most important are changes from high to low atmospheric pressure, or vice versa. In addition, the weight of an abundant snowfall creates a temporary "high pressure" under the ice, which frequently activates the fish. A strong spell of low pressure with mild weather can melt snow on the ice and provide more light for the fish to hunt by.

A permanent and stable weather pattern has two effects. First, the good fishing at the onset of the pattern gradually tapers off. Secondly, the pike show increasingly predictable periods of biting as the weather stabilizes and persists for a considerable time. These biting periods are also shifted gradually during the winter as the days grow longer and brighter.

Towards spring, the earth's increasing warmth and the greater sunshine raise the water temperature. This stimulates the activity of creatures in the water – especially along the shores, in reed banks and at brook mouths. Hordes of stonefly larvae now float up to the ice's lower edges and slowly climb through the cracks that form in the ice. These insects are a welcome food supplement for many small fish that follow

the larvae's ascent. The small fish activity in turn attracts the attention of pike, which may then become hasty and make an easy catch for any fisherman who is on the spot. For the same reason, out in the depths of lakes and archipelagos, the activity is high around shoals and isles or on pondweed bottoms. Perch, too, obey the rule. Whereas roaches and other whitefish focus on fly larvae, shrimp and crustaceans, the perch at such places are ever more occupied with hunting tiny fish. And predatory pike are certainly prowling about, as they never give up a good area for hunting.

The pike's biting periods

All that can be said with certainty about the pike's biting periods during the winter is that they occur. And indeed they do, with an amazing precision in timing. But one cannot generalize much farther than that. There are fishermen who definitely speak of the "eleven o'clock bite", the "bite at two", the "morning bite" or "dusk bite" and so on. Nonetheless, so many factors play a role and influence the pike's hunting and feeding habits throughout a long winter that only during short and, in particular, stable intervals of weather can one lean back with some degree of assurance about when the next biting period will come.

The same may be said for the length and quality of biting periods. If they happen at all during a fishing day, they can vary from several hours to only some ten minutes long. Likewise, the intensity of bites – how many occur during a given period – differs as well. There may be a flurry of bites for limited periods during one day, while the following day brings fewer and more cautious bites. It is also interesting that the possible biting periods can differ between fishermen on the same lake during the same day. Whereas one fisherman may think he has caught plenty of pike almost continuously except, perhaps, in the morning and late afternoon, another fisherman may report just the opposite: that the fish were biting enthusiastically during the morning and towards evening in spite of nothing happening for the rest of the day. Such differences are usually easy to explain by analyzing where in the lake these fishermen have had their respective experiences. It frequently turns out that those who fished deep all day had the good day-time fishing, and those who only walked along the shallows near shore got their fish early or late in the day. It can then be concluded that the pike hunted shallow at first,

A clever tactic can be to get out on the ice before dawn. Then you will not miss a possible biting period as the sky brightens.

moved out to the depths, and finally returned towards land in the evening.

The fact that pike sometimes have very distinctive biting periods is soon learned by adept ice-fishermen. For a new-comer to the game, it is a fascinating experience to see one set of gear after the other fall down. Within a few minutes, enormous activity may erupt at a fishing spot where nothing has happened for several hours. Equally astonishing is that the biting period on such occasions often stops as sharply as it began. It may end after 10 intensive minutes as easily as after 30 minutes or a couple of hours. It may start early in the morning, just at dawn, or else it may wait until the sun stands at the zenith. It may go on from 9:10 until 11:30 AM, or between 8 and 9 AM and again between 1 and 2:30 PM. By contrast, intensive bites may occur during the morning and die out totally after lunch.

Some days offer no biting period whatever, either because they are just dull days or because the fish only take a casual bite now and then. Other days, however, may display three very clear biting periods – in the morning, at lunchtime and at dusk – with occasional, irregular casual bites in between. If the morning brings an early biting period, for example, from 8:30 until 10:00 AM, followed by a dead calm, it usually means that a quite distinctive biting period will come in the afternoon too.

Part of the joy of fishing is that we can never be entirely sure what awaits us. A good example of this is provided by a visit I made to an inland lake at the beginning of March a few winters ago. The expedition was aimed primarily at pikeperch, so my companion – the artist Johan Kölare – and I had loaded up mainly with small and medium-size roaches. These were sunk to the bottom in a channel that normally holds some winter pikeperch. The first rods were set out before dawn, already at 7:30 AM. By 9 AM and broad daylight, nothing had happened and we decided to set out more rods – mine in the shallower areas with 4-7 metres of water, and Johan's where it was a bit deeper at 8-10 metres. We had now peppered the channel with a total of 15 rods and, being impatient, were actually starting to wonder if we should pick them up and change the location, since not a single encouraging contact had come our way. We resolved, though, to give it another 45 minutes.

And that was lucky, for suddenly at 9:30 everything changed. The "fishless" channel came alive with fish, biting all over. Within several minutes I had bites on all eight of my rods at the same time! Of course, I was far from keeping up with them. The rush of bites stopped 55 minutes later, as abruptly as it had begun. We got a welcome pause, and a chance to load our rods again. During the rush, we had counted more than 30 bites. It was as if heaven had opened up, after the two morning hours of unusual sluggishness. In fact, this was exactly what did happen. After an overcast morning with almost black storm clouds, the sun had broken through at the very moment when the biting period commenced. It had done so with such energy that the four-inch-thick white rug of snow, onto which we had walked at dawn, was now turned into large patches of pure slush.

While we recovered and contemplated this phenomenon, we also had reason to wonder how the fish's frantic activity could stop so quickly. During the hour or more that followed, it was once again as though the entire channel had died. Not one bite came, or a sign that any of the baits were stressed in the typical way that sometimes warns of a bite. Thus we began to settle in for a long, uncertain wait. But the story repeated itself. After the dead interval, the sky might as well have opened anew, as unexpectedly as a couple of hours earlier. For 45 minutes we had a hectic job, with around 20 bites on somewhat fewer rods. Then another 90 minutes of complete calm descended. Finally we faced the day's last biting period, which lasted only 15 minutes at 2:30-2:45 PM and yielded six bites.

In sum, therefore, about 60 bites befell us during three periods with a combined length of 120 minutes. The bites were distributed with a slight emphasis on pike, about 35, the remainder being pikeperch. Yet no more than four pikeperch had landed up on the ice. The others had spat out their bait while we were occupied with bites elsewhere. Pike tend to be less finicky, and we had managed to land 16 of them, 15 being returned to the water.

Under conditions with more time available for each individual bite, the catch would have been much greater. But this day was not a normal one, and the bites came faster than the time allowed. Besides, the catch that we got was more than sufficient. Here is an example leading to the subject of "fish-ing with intelligence". Undeniably, the ice-fisherman or ice-angler who uses many rods can sometimes make considerable catches of pike, and a risk of overfishing the stock arises in small and sensitive waters. Hence, we must learn the difficult art of stopping soon enough, or learn correct ways of returning the fish, if we want to maintain the good fishing in these waters. The criticism which is occasionally directed against traditional winter ice-fishing concerns just such large catches of pike that occur now and then.

The introduction to this chapter dealt with biting periods. Having observed that such periods can vary widely in both timing and quality, we are in a position to see what maximizes the fisherman's chances of foreseeing a catch: one must spend time regularly on the ice and thereby know a bit about how the possible biting pattern will look at the moment of fishing.

Problems in high winter

All sportfishing contains an inherent element of capriciousness and unpredictability. However skilful we may be, we thus often fall short, especially when confronted by new difficulties. Pike fishing in the high winter is, on several accounts, harder – as well as more interesting – than the fishing we do on the first and last ices of winter.

Unfortunately, many ice-fishermen stop angling in high winter. The reasons seem to be numerous: that the ice has become too thick and heavy for drilling, that too much snow lies on it, that the increasing cold causes trouble with constant freezing of the ice holes, and that the pike are less easy to find in shallow water than during the early winter.

Regarding the first problem, accumulation of ice: this is directly related to the fishing method and to how the ice holes are made. In traditional ice-fishing, it is recommended that the holes be about 30 cm in diameter, due to the complications that can occur when using a large hook. Such big holes cannot be made without an ice pick or ice drill. In thick ice, some effort is naturally required to cut holes of this size in the ice repeatedly during a fishing day when looking for pike. But when practising a more modern type of ice-angling, as described in the present book – with the large hook replaced by an ordinary angling hook – this problem is eliminated. A plain 150-200 mm ice drill can now do the whole job quickly and smoothly even in ice of normal thickness.

As for the second complication, snow, not much can be

An ice pick is effective, but it can still be tiring to hack holes through strong ice time and again for a whole day.

done about it. Most tiring in this case, perhaps, is the need to trudge through deep snow. However, it might be possible to find a less distant fishing spot.

The complications of cold can be coped with as well. Constantly going round and sprinkling a little warm water in the ice holes is the commonest, and most tedious, procedure. When extreme cold prevails, this becomes a continuous chore. A classic trick, which at least prevents the ice from freezing around the fishing line, is to slice up and thread a reed around the line in a hole. Another trick is to pour snow into the hole – preferably flaky, airy snow that does not sink fast. Also effective is to pour a little alcohol in the hole, and then a little snow on top to keep the alcohol from evaporating too rapidly. Likewise, drops of vegetable or animal (fish) oil can be added to the hole and stop it from freezing up.

The last problem, that the pike tend toward deeper water in high winter, need not mean that the shallow coves are completely dead. On the contrary, certain coves and shallow habitats have such a special biotope that they harbour pike all winter long. Not seldom, really big pike can be found in these places.

Search strategies

With all due respect for relaxation and recreation, the ultimate point of fishing is to catch fish. This is why we are ready to withstand bad weather and hours of zealous effort. Few other leisure passions match the undoubted power of sportfishing to give its practitioners enormous returns for their pains.

In reality, the yield and the pleasure of fishing grow fast with one's experience and skill. Only when we feel that we are beginning to master certain methods, techniques and problems does the deep, true joy of fishing become manifest. Then we recognize that an interest in fishing is worth taking seriously, no matter which form of fishing we attempt. It is also then that we become genuinely stimulated by fresh challenges and difficulties, so that the fishing begins to acquire other qualities than the simple quantity of results.

Pike should be sought at varying depths during the winter. The general pattern is that, immediately after the ice is laid, and for some time thereafter, the pike swim rather shallowly – in coves and on bottoms of medium depth. In larger and deeper lakes, the fishing is often done fairly close to shore.

On the other hand, during high winter the pike frequently move out to significant depths, even into the "free water" far from land. Still, a fisherman who can cope with all the obstacles of thick ice, freezing in holes, and lots of snow, and who also has enough line on his fishing rod or ice-angling gear, will have many enjoyable hours of fishing in midwinter – often at depths between 10 and 20 metres, on deep heels and cliffs, and sometimes out along flat bottoms in the vicinity of structures.

Structures

Structures consist of everything that is not sterile and uniform. They exist both above and below the water surface. From visible structures above water, we can frequently deduce potential or probable structures under water. A headland that projects far out will presumably be prolonged as an underwater ridge. A flat field on one side of a lake reveals that there may be shallow bottoms, perhaps full of pondweed, outside the large reeds that begin where the field ends. Steep mountains that fall straight into the water can show which side of the lake is deepest. A group of small islets is a possible sign of interesting projections and uneven areas near them, and so on.

Pike are not typical free-water fish like, for instance, pikeperch. The pike seeks environments that offer it camouflage and holding places, where it can sneak around without being noticed. Underwater ridges, cliffs that connect shallow and deep waters, plateaus and rises, sunken rocks and deep coves, around small islets, in deep channels, on slopes outside large reed beds and stream mouths – these are examples of environments with irregular structures where it often pays to look for pike in high winter. But since the pike even at this time make repeated visits to shallow and plant-rich shores, we should follow some kind of strategy when searching for them.

When the bites start

Eventually you begin to get bites – and quite possibly on the rod that is farthest in toward shore, just when you find yourself farthest out, to make things a little harder. But after a few more bites, you can usually discern a pattern. It might be that the bites occur only on rods which are 75-125 metres from

Suggested strategies

As pike fishermen, we have an inclination towards visible structures. If we are also devoted to spinning and baitcasting, we also automatically head for relatively shallow environments. The consequence is often that, even in high winter, the ice-fishing or ice-angling becomes too confined to shallow, inshore places which the pike have abandoned. In other words, we fish at the wrong spots, although we may suspect that we ought to try fishing deeper.

Leave the shore and fish at the cliffs

A simple but very fruitful strategy is usually to move out from the shore as if "blindly". Somewhere along the way, the water will get deeper – you encounter a deep edge or a deeper bottom where the pike prefer to linger. It may be 30, 50, or 150 metres outside the shallow reeds.

This approach can be applied regardless of whether you fish in a large channel or a big cove, or just walk straight out on an open bay or lake. The principle is elementary: instead of beginning to fish by horizontally following a strip of land on relatively shallow water, set up your rods in a straight line going outward – be it on a lake, a cove, across a bay or channel, or whatever! If nothing happens, keep moving the rods in the same direction, or else choose a new place and do the same thing. Once a few such straight "scratches" have been made at different locations, and you have seen how the fishing improves, your sport will be more interesting and dynamic.

Increase the distance between the rods

The same strategy is used to advantage when moving on all kinds of large, unknown waters. It is primarily a matter of trying to locate the productive fishing places. Without an echo-sounder, depth charts, or previous experience of the water we are

This high-winter pike took the hook at a cliff outside a cove, where the bottom sloped from five to nine metres down.

Blue echo-sounder of "Flashlight model": This little hand-held echo-sounder from Bios gives quick depth readouts even through strong ice.

on, there is often good sense in increasing the separation of the rods, so as to cover a larger area. Instead of stationing the rods straight outward at intervals of 8-10 metres, one can wisely double the distance to about 20 metres. An important point is to place all the rods so that one can easily see a bite on any of them while one is moving across the ice. Nor should one forget to measure the depth when sounding at each new ice hole. This allows one to check continually whether the water is becoming deeper or shallower.

Echo-sounder

For the ice-angler who wants to exploit the short days of winter with full efficiency, an echo-sounder may be helpful. With this instrument, one can scan through the ice and determine both the bottom structures and the occurrence of fish. On large waters, it is then easier to find underwater rocks and deep edges, compared to drilling and sounding manually. Moreover, when you use an echo-sounder with a display terminal, you can detect preyfish – and where there are preyfish, there are also predatory fish!

Whenever we have a chance to choose, it is time to experiment with different baits! Perch often work as well as roach.

land. Then you can either wait awhile to confirm that the pattern is steady, or immediately start to move some other rods toward the active area. These rods should be placed horizontally at the same depth, to the sides of the rods where the activity has occurred.

If the bites occur only on a couple of rods standing farthest out, you may as well move everything to that location, since the fish seem to be lingering there. No one has said that the sport is for lazy bones!

Varying the presentation of bait

We fishermen have a tendency to become conservative in our methods. Once a rhythm has struck us that we are satisfied with, it is easy to get stuck in our behaviour. It soon becomes a process of "this manoeuvre", "that colour" and the like. When choosing the prey for winter fishing, though, not many stereotypes exist to get stuck with, since the range is naturally quite restricted. In addition, we are often content to obtain some live bait at all, so the stereotypes can be forced upon us by a lack of alternatives. And if we cannot get live bait, dead bait must do. Even a herring fillet – without the head – may work wonders in the tiniest freshwater lake when the pike are hungry.

As the pike is such an all-round eater, it sometimes enjoys the luxury of being selective and finicky. In certain waters where a particular type of prey is abundant, the pike are naturally imprinted by it, but even here an unusual prey can suddenly prove to be what brings the greatest triumph.

Concentration on the task. With the line between your fingers, it is easy to feel when the pike chews and turns the roach.

Thus, if you have access to very different baits such as perch, large roach, small roach, crucian carp, and smelt, it can be worth experimenting. Nor is this surprising, since we know how selective and variable the pike can be about artificial baits – as regards their sizes, models, liveliness and colours. A systematic fisherman soon gets an idea of whether the pike prefer one kind or another during a given day.

The bait's presentation over the bottom can also be varied. A common recommendation is to let the bait hang 30-50 centimetres over the bottom, since both the pike and the preyfish tend to stay near the bottom in winter. But if you are fishing shallow – at less than 4 metres – a good tactic can be to place the bait at a medium depth, where it may be easier for pike to notice and identify from greater distances as well. If nothing

else, it is useful to present the bait high up under spring ice, as the small fish swim in higher water layers and sometimes just below the ice. At such times, angling only one or two metres down, in water that may be 10-15 metres deep, can feel a bit strange; but such doubts soon disappear. The predatory fish are usually quite clear about where the food is!

The strike

As long as pike angling is done with small, sharp hooks, you do not need to make a strong strike of the kind that sportfishermen are often seen practising when baitcasting. For angling with a rod, it is enough to lift the rod decisively in an arc so as to hook a pike. The same is true in wintertime if a rod is used.

However, when the angling is done with converted ice-fishing gear that has been rigged for angling, the technique is somewhat different. Here the pike must be caught manually, without the help offered by a rod's long strong action. But a rod is not necessary anyhow. A pike that is moving after turning the baitfish in the usual manner can easily be hooked by pausing briefly when the pike is still swimming and has the whole baitfish in its jaws. The normally successful hooking is then made perfectly in one corner of the mouth. In directed pike fishing, of course, a steel wire is used and you need not worry that the stop or strike will be too hard.

If the pike is not swimming noticeably when you judge that the time has come to hook it, a more definite strike should be made. This is done by pinching the line at the same moment as you jerk upward with your hand. It is important to be sure that you have immediate contact with the pike when making the strike. When angling with a long rod, a pike can be hooked even if a wrong judgment leaves a couple of metres of slack in the line. This margin of error shrinks considerably when the strike must be done by hand. Half a metre of slack line is often enough to miss a fish that is being hand-hooked.

When the pike angling is done with a steel wire, one need seldom be afraid of a line break during the strike. But the same cannot be said when angling with a nylon leader. The 0.50-mm nylon leader that is preferably used on perch and pikeperch, for example, will snap in an instant if the strike on a pike is done wrong – that is, too brutally when the line also lies wrong in the pike's jaws.

Thus, the strike is a critical point when you angle with a nylon leader, and it should therefore be carried out in a cor-

Roach baited with two-hook tackle on ice-fishing gear, with a pike in the foreground / Slide BB: Tackle with two hooks is very effective for hooking pike at an early stage. But this tackle should not be used when the leader consists of nylon line, as the tackle then inevitably gets tangled in a pike's sharp teeth.

rect and well-judged manner: neither too abruptly and hard, nor too loosely and softly, but somewhere between these extremes. A fisherman who learns to make well-balanced strikes can achieve impressive results. My own "all-time record" is 121 pike in a row without any broken leader, when fishing with a 0.50-mm nylon leader and a treble hook.

Many anglers enjoy using a bait tackle that has two treble hooks instead of one. The first hook is placed in the baitfish's spinal region, and the other in the region of the head.

Playing the fish

After striking and hooking the pike, you have to deal with the playing and the finale. Eager and unaccustomed fishermen, who may otherwise be talented at smooth strikes, are unfor-tunately prone to losing many a hook and fish while playing a pike. They are not prepared either for the pike's sudden, powerful shakes, or for its violent rushes which can become ever worse as the pike is forced closer to the ice roof and, at last, into the hole. At these critical moments, zeal and a fear of losing the fish often take the upper hand, and one's grip on the line – which should now soften and let slip – becomes hard and cramped. A leader lying among the pike's teeth is then snapped off, unless it is made of wire.

Instead, the playing should be carried out decisively so that a certain pressure is constantly on the fish, giving it no time to rest, at the same time as one remains alert to parry the pike's stronger outbursts and shakes of the head by let-ting out line and allowing one's arms to act as a sensitive rod tip.

Large winter pike

Sooner or later, there it is, when one least expects it. The peak of pikes. And how the story will end is as exciting as uncertain.

No statistics are kept on the total number of large pike that are landed upon the ice every winter. This must be mainly because winter pike are caught by the usual method, with ice-fishing gear and hook, and that the catch is consequently not considered truly appropriate to sportfishing by the prevailing definitions. The Swedish Sportfishing Association is the only agency in its country that registers large fish, but their catch must fulfil carefully stipulated requirements in order to be approved eventually for registration. The Association provides special application forms for this purpose.

Pike weighing over 12 kg that are caught with ice-fishing gear and then played by hand do not satisfy these requirements since the equipment is not counted as hand equipment. As a result, such big pike are not registered, and knowledge of them frequently goes no farther than the person who caught them and any witnesses. If the pike is really gigantic, it may be mentioned in the local press. Occasional enormous pike are also noted in the sportfishing press. But certainly there are many big pike each winter that get caught without public attention. How numerous the unrecorded cases are is open to speculation.

As a devoted practitioner of ice-angling and modern angling, I sometimes run into ice-fishermen of various sorts and exchange the kind of information that sportfishing enthusiasts trade wherever they meet. Even if only half of these reports are true, they convince me that quite a lot of very big pike are caught from the ice each winter.

Surprisingly often, it seems to be almost total amateurs in the field who succeed at such feats. They are people who angle once every three years when in the countryside, at their club waters, or the like, and commonly on waters where fishing for pike is normally sparse. One conclusion is that "ordinary folks" gladly indulge in the special charm and excitement of ice-fishing. But another may be that, if more "sportfishermen" were to concentrate on the opportunities offered by winter pike, the registry of big fish would receive far more new annual entries.

Most of the winter's large pike are still caught with a traditional angling hook, by fishermen who are often deficiently equipped. Here was a narrow escape to success.

When I hear such stories, and know at the same time how many big pike I myself have lost while ice-fishing, it is also tempting to ask how many big pike are lost for every one that is landed. How many snapped lines from ice-fishing gear? How many bitten off? How many worn away on sharp ice edges? How many times have the ice holes been too small? How often has an ice pick, or experience with using it properly, been lacking? How many lines have been drilled or chopped off in attempts to make the hole larger?

Questions abound, but one that I have long sought the answer to is whether directed fishing can be pursued for big pike on the winter ice. Today I would reply without hesitation: yes! And for any fisherman who makes an effort on the right water, a big one is within reach.

Directed fishing for big winter pike

All industrious sportfishermen make bonus catches and acquire bonus experiences at times. We catch fish that we were not looking for, or did not even think were in the water, and we make other unexpected and often pleasant encounters of diverse kinds. Such episodes which I would call bonuses concern big pike – over 5 kg in weight. Generally, winter fishing through the years has yielded a greater percentage of big pike in my waters than other seasons have. This is true even on waters where I have not primarily been fishing for pike.

Much the same apparently applies to a lot of inland lakes. Where the fishing relatively seldom produces big pike with more conventional sportfishing methods – at any rate in terms of the quantities caught – great numbers often result when the fishing is done from the ice.

On the whole, winter fishing from the ice, despite its limitations and a fair share of fashion, has advantages over pike fishing in open waters during other seasons. For example, it is frequently needless to ring in so-called "hot" areas to succeed with winter fishing. For one of the main benefits to winter fishing is the fact that very little pike fishing is done in winter, compared with the summer half-year's activity on this front. A winter angler thus almost always walks on undisturbed fishing spots.

So many factors make winter fishing difficult that it can seem absolutely miraculous for pike of this size to come up on the ice as often as they do.

Everybody who has fished much for pike knows how important it can be to arrive first at an undisturbed place – and the odds of succeeding are boosted substantially if it is also the right place. When fishing in winter, the pike as a rule have been living at peace for a period of up to several months, and welcome the arrival of tempting meals that are easy to catch. This goes far to compensate a winter pike fisherman for the more mobile boat fishing of the summer half-year.

Neither do you need to set up ten, or even five, rods to succeed. Three or four which are moved regularly can be enough. Moreover, the winter catch is promoted by actively seeking the fish. If you also have a previous acquaintance with the fishing place, you will get a fish sooner or later even when using nothing but a rod.

Besides, big pike themselves are active during the winter. They have routes and hunting routines that are more distinctive as they become older and larger. They also often have clearly defined biting periods. A pike fisherman who makes frequent trips to the water and spends the entire winter day there, from dawn to dusk, will learn a great deal about pike behaviour and biting periods.

There is considerable research to show that metabolism and growth in fish are much lower in winter than in summer. This finding is equally valid for pike, even though they are more comfortable with cold weather than many other species are. But despite the relatively low intake and processing of food by pike in winter, this certainly does not mean they take no interest in food.

On several occasions, especially in the archipelagos, I have caught pike in high winter that were stuffed full of newly eaten fish. The most striking example occurred on a bay in the southern archipelago of Stockholm. That day, we caught 18 pike in the bay and, since nearly all of them were taut and hard around their bellies, we investigated a couple of the fattest specimens. They contained bream, ide, large and small roach, perch, burbot and Baltic herring – a menu that obviously explained why this bay yielded so many pike in February. And we had the pleasure of arriving in the midst of their feast while it was still going on.

Hence I am able to confirm that pike can be not only active during winter, but very active. They have no hesitation in gobbling the baitfish which are offered, and they often put up resistance with a tenacity and conditioning that may greatly exceed the state of both spring and autumn pike.

To be sure, the pike have sluggish intervals when they stand and collect parasites – occasionally for several weeks, and notably during periods of persistent high atmospheric pressure with much snow on the ice, or when the sunshine is rather constant. But the normal pattern for pike is that they have a "weather temper" and alternate strongly between periods of high and low activity. Winter is no exception in this regard.

Summary

Pike are big game from the ice during almost the whole winter. It is perfectly feasible to pursue directed fishing for big pike, too, since one soon finds out which places tend to yield large specimens.

To my great satisfaction I could say, when writing in March 2000, that pike fishing from winter ice was at last becoming really popular. That winter, large numbers of beautiful specimens were caught. Well-known and otherwise successful pike specialists had continued to hear out my enthusiasm for ice-angling in recent years. Stefan Trumstedt, one of our most skilful pike fishermen on open waters, probably set a kind of new record with the magnificent giant of 14.8 kg which he angled on the ice of an archipelago bay at on 29 January. Presumably this was just the beginning of the trend.

Losing big pike on the ice

The outcome of an encounter with big pike is always uncertain, particularly in the context of ice-fishing, and not least when the fisherman is unaccustomed as well as lacking assistance or a gaff. There are many ways of losing a big pike. What follow are some examples from the repertoire of those lost by myself and other fishermen of my acquaintance.

Too short a line

My first contacts with very big winter pike all went wrong as far as I was concerned. At that time I used traditional ice-fishing gear, with reels carrying the classic blue spun line. But instead of an angling hook, I had an ordinary Mustad treble hook, the leader being an 0.80-mm nylon line.

Two initial encounters with the archipelago's crocodiles were rather similar. I had set up four rods, baited them with live perch, and moved ever farther away from them as I looked for more perch. When I noticed a rod falling, I began to run like

This time it went well, but a fine set of fishing equipment is not always enough to land a big pike with.

crazy across the ice. But already before getting there, I could see the gear – whose reel turned ever faster as the line spun off it – suddenly being jerked up and slammed down across the ice hole. On both occasions, the fresh blue line had simply been snapped off like sewing thread next to the line spool.

Too weak a leader

The remedy against a repeat performance was to lengthen the line with another 35 metres of nylon line, 0.35-0.40 mm in diameter. This led to new discoveries: several pike were caught, but with equally depressing results when it came to holding such big locomotives!

By then I had developed a technique that aimed at frightening away the pike once they took the bait – by running toward the gear, which naturally sent them flying. The purpose of scaring them was to be able to hook them at an early stage, in flight as it were, before they had a chance to swallow the bait, so that I could return them. For this reason I used fairly large treble hooks of size 2 or 1/0. The method is effective insofar as the pike is usually hooked well and is easy to get loose. But when it comes to really big pike of 10 kg or more, the weakest link is mercilessly revealed.

The high speed attained by a big pike when it is frightened in this manner, combined with its substantial weight, now had the result that my 0.80-mm leader was what went off. Just when I prepared to hook the fish, there was a feeling of massive weight, the nylon line cut a couple of millimetres into my forefinger joint, and a "snap" was the last I heard of the leader.

I wasted three big pike before I learned that the key is to use steel wire. Actually I would have used it to begin with, but for a vague and stubborn notion that a nylon leader could catch more fish because of its relative transparency. In those days I still believed that pike are suspicious of visible steel wires.

Too little luck

But sometimes not even a steel-wire leader is sufficient. Two of my absolutely biggest winter pike have been lost in other ways. One of them suddenly got tired of the game after awhile, and rushed without any apology straight into the reeds 20 metres away. Whoever has played a large pike that puts up a solid fight – as winter pike almost always do – knows what I mean. Unfortunately the fish proceeded to tangle itself so well in there that I could not draw it out again.

My fishing companion Kjell Appelgren had better luck when a female pike of no less than 13.2 kg did the same thing. She turned back out of, and into, the reeds not once but twice, before Kjell could set the gaff in her jaw hook and bring her up on the ice.

Backlash

Among the elementary principles of ice-fishing gear is that one must learn to keep an eye on the loose line while playing the fish.

But before getting that far, one has to hook the fish in the proper way. And the main point here is to avoid a backlash on the reel while hooking. Backlash is caused when you pull excessively in relation to the length of loose line that should first have been drawn off the reel.

Among my most embarrassing examples of how to lose a big pike occurred together with an inexperienced companion named Lazlo. On this day he was to be initiated into fishing tricks for the winter. A fish took the bait, but did not pull any line after the rod fell. When we got there, the line just extended limply down into the hole.

The ice had a foot of snow on it and the water was two metres deep. An alert pike should have swum away as we approached the hole, I thought, and drew the hasty conclusion that it was a little pike which had bitten and then spat out. I had no idea that it might be a big pike acting so passively, since I was still unaware that this very behaviour is sometimes typical of big pike. A large pike has no need to turn a small baitfish. It merely glides forward and closes its sizable jaws over the bait. Then it often lingers at the site of the crime until it swallows. Only after that does it begin to take line. But I had not yet learned these details.

As I gripped the line to feel it a bit, it started to move – first slowly, then ever faster. I tried to keep loose line ahead of it, showing the novice how a strike is made, but the fish continued to speed up and I misjudged the amount of loose line that was ahead. The consequence of such a strike is a backlash of the worst sort, followed by chaos.

At one end of the line, five or six metres away below the ice, was a very heavy old pike swinging back and forth violently. Above the ice at the other end, my arm swung back and forth in tune with the pike. I held the line hard so that Lazlo would have a chance to unravel the backlash, but this backlash was worse than usual and he had no experience. The big pike stopped shaking, took off and simply broke the line. Before the winter's supreme match had really begun, it was over.

Tackle and equipment for pike

Two things are of overwhelming importance when angling for pike from the ice: sufficient length of fishing line, and steel wire for a leader! Apart from these, it matters less whether the actual fishing occurs with some kind of rod having a reel, or with a variant of ice-fishing gear. However, I would emphasize that a fisherman who wants to get his catch formally approved as a sport-fishing feat must use a rod and reel. More about how to equip oneself for pike can be found in the chapter on equipment.

Pikeperch
(Lucio Perca)

Being out on the snow-covered winter ice during a sparkling, starry, windless morning before daylight is an experience of a special kind. The silence and darkness are palpable, as is the almost sensual cold on your face when you climb out of a warm car. Then there are the sounds of movement – low squishes from your boots on the soft snow, the crackling noise from tramping on hard snow, the sled's smooth hiss as you pull it over snow and ice, and the rhythmical whisper of synthetic material on your body. Perhaps a resounding in the ice, or a tawny owl's hooting, breaks the calm from one of the black, jagged silhouettes of the shores and rolls across the frozen surface.

From the viewpoint of sportfishing, an early start to the day can also be a good tactic when you try to get in touch with pikeperch. During the winter, pikeperch are most often active by day; but since they sometimes hunt at dawn, it is worth getting out in time in order not to miss this opportunity.

For the same reason it can be rewarding to stay on the ice during the first dark hour of late day. When fishing at dusk, I have seen such intensive rushes of biting that they continued until it was completely dark. On one occasion, the darkness was so dense when the fishing stopped that my equipment had to be left on the ice.

The next day, there may be no activity whatever at the same fishing spot. Not because all the fish were caught yesterday, or because the weather has changed. Perhaps the pikeperch have simply moved, or are not in a good mood at the moment. Pikeperch are mysterious fish, and a challenge for whoever wants to depart from old ruts.

It is quite proper that pikeperch and their habits still carry an aura of myth and mystique. Moreover, it is logical that a catch of pikeperch is frequently made as a pure bonus during directed fishing for some other species.

Below and opposite: An early start to the fishing day is sometimes the decisive tactic. This specimen of 4.5 kg bit distinctively outside a small headland just before sunrise.

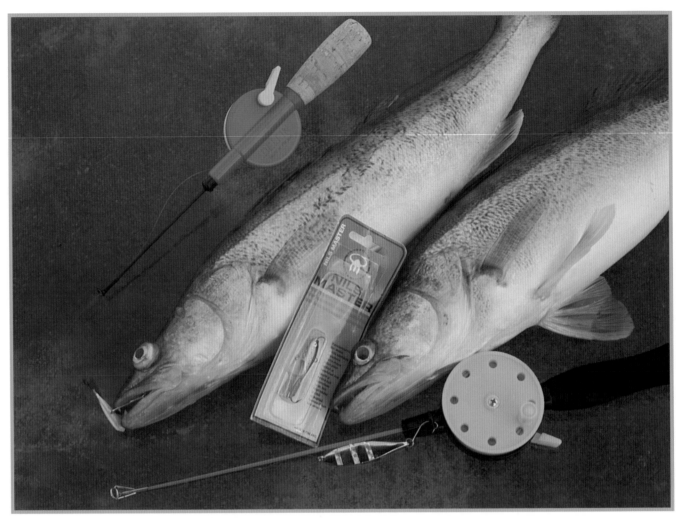

The traditional way of fishing for pikeperch in winter employs large vertical, or balance, pirks of the Nils Master type. This ice-fishing often yields small specimens, but can still be a pleasant supplement to ice-angling.

Few sportfishermen manage to catch a pikeperch during the summer, which is considered to be the normal season for such fishing. Still fewer, of course, are those who have succeeded in wintertime. But the present chapter will hopefully enable pikeperch to become more than a rare bonus catch – rather, a possible and even probable catch for those who adjust their sights well. Winter is a good time for luring pikeperch!

The pikeperch's body form is not built for lightning attacks. Its relative slowness is compensated, though, by excellent ability to see in the dark. Without this, a pikeperch would have great difficulty in holding its own as a predator and soon be outcompeted by others, such as pike. In murky waters and poor light, its well-developed visual sense is shown to advan-

tage. Under these conditions the pikeperch can fully exploit its special hunting technique, which involves slowly pursuing and approaching a prey without being noticed. Then it does not matter so much that the pikeperch is a bit slow and clumsy. The prey often discovers it too late to escape.

Pikeperch have a strong predilection for dim visibility conditions – those that offer advantages for hunting. The fish's survival as both a species and an individual, not to mention its distribution, depends on the possibility of exploiting poor illumination. In murky waters, pikeperch may be active all day round, whereas in clear waters it tends to become more active during the darker parts of the day. Interestingly, too, in clear waters it is often very active by day when there is cloudy weather or twilight. This is especially true in wintertime.

Pikeperch as a winter fish

Fishing for pikeperch is usually associated with summer sun and warmth. There is hardly a pikeperch fisherman who has not been out on a balmy summer evening between May and August. Thus, angling for pikeperch from the ice during winter goes against most of the myths and perceptions that still surround this fish. No season is farther than winter from the heat waves of midyear – and yet the pikeperch actively invite the angler throughout winter! I can confidently say so after a number of winters spent on directed angling for pikeperch from ice, which have yielded over a hundred specimens. And similar fishing luck has befallen my companions on lakes of various sizes as well as in archipelago bays.

The fact is that pikeperch are among our most successful predatory fish. As such, they naturally continue to hunt during the winter. Why not? Being able to see in the dark, they have a great advantage over other fish in the winter half-year's low light. In lakes with stocks of ruff or small perch, these may be the main food, and then the pikeperch's attention is chiefly focused on the bottom. In other waters, roach or smelt may be the basis of their diet, as sand lances and herring may be in the archipelagos. At all events, it can be assumed that pikeperch, like pike, are fairly flexible and will eat whatever is at hand if it looks edible – such as a pirk.

My own experience with traditional ice-fishing for pikeperch is unfortunately quite limited. I can boast of only a few fish caught in this way. But since I have angled for pikeperch in parallel with devoted ice-fishermen, there have been numerous opportunities to compare our methods. At the risk of seeming to favour my particular approach, as I obviously do, it is evident that ice-fishing usually catches small-grown pikeperch. Angling with natural bait does not yield fewer, but primarily larger, specimens. In effect, angling weeds out the small ones at the same time as it apparently attracts bigger ones. On the other hand, to be honest, I have not yet met any traditional pikeperch ice-fisherman who uses pirks that match the format of the baitfish, about 12-18 cm long, which I would recommend for winter pikeperch angling.

The pikeperch's temperament

Like all other fish, the pikeperch is easy to catch when it is in good form, but much trickier at other times. To succeed regularly with pikeperch during winter angling, one must keep in mind that this fish has a peculiar temperament. The more familiar the latter becomes, the better your catches will be!

A traditional ice-fisherman seeking pikeperch in wintertime does not notice the fish's changes of temperament as readily as anglers do. Either he gets a bite eventually or he doesn't. Occasionally he may feel that something perch-like down there made the pirk lift cautiously for a moment, with no sequel. Or else, a long while later, he may suddenly get a hard bite in the same hole that nearly tears the rod out of his hand. Here the ice-fisherman has an advantage over anglers. Even when the pikeperch are not interested in food, a relatively good catch can result, since an attractive bait may release a reflex to attack so that the pikeperch hooks itself.

For an angler, however, reflexive attacks are not enough. To be hooked by angling, a pikeperch must be made both to turn the bait and to take it fully into the jaws. Under sluggish conditions, a pikeperch angler may miss the fish even though he gets at least as many bites as an ice-fisherman. This is because the pikeperch gladly spits out the bait when it is sluggish. Nonetheless, an experienced angler can coax the fish and use special tricks that often bring success even when the conditions are bad. These tricks will be discussed later below.

The art of angling pikeperch from ice

A pikeperch in good form behaves as a veritable predator and, from the standpoint of an unsentimental observer, just about as insanely as all other kinds of predatory fish when in such form. It is mobile, goal-directed, and unhealthily interested in anything that moves – all of which makes it comparatively catchable. Its bite on a live baitfish is decisive and clear. Right after the bite, the pikeperch takes the line at high speed. An angler needs only to wait 15-20 seconds before hooking the pikeperch in the middle of its rush. By then, the baitfish is often halfway down in its stomach. If the pikeperch is to be returned to the water, the hooking should be done rather quickly before it has time to swallow.

The rare occasions when a winter pikeperch displays this mood are the ones where it seriously bites even on large hooks. A fisherman's best way of hooking it is then to reach the spot fast and make a strike before it spits out the bait.

Pikeperch are very keen on eating smelt and, when in fine form, will nip the prey from all directions before swallowing it fast.

There are lakes with such a rich stock of pikeperch that fishing with a large hook, and even with dead herring, regularly yields a catch. One might thus be led to believe that the traditional ice-fishing gear is proper equipment for pikeperch. But this is not the case.

The traditional gear with its large hook is, and remains, primarily for pike. By contrast, pikeperch can be extremely cautious, and tackle which is accepted by pike will often be totally useless for pikeperch. Under normal conditions, and in water with better than normal stocks of pikeperch, the winter's angling for pikeperch is therefore a lot less straightforward than pike fishing.

At first, winter pikeperch may be a little hard for newcomers to understand. But even pike fishermen who consider themselves adept, and are accustomed to traditional ice-fishing with a signal cork, have much to learn when it comes to pikeperch. For this is by no means an indolent sort of fishing.

In fact, a pikeperch's stealthy biting in wintertime can happen so softly and carefully that most fishermen never discover the phenomenon, because they fish with insufficient concentration or are too busy with other matters on the ice, such as being sociable, and rely too heavily on their technology and bite indicators.

On the level where fishing for pikeperch should be conducted, it is something of an art of concentration, where one must be "on the ball" in the same sense as other kinds of fishermen must if they want to avoid losing too many fish. Realization of this can lead to rich rewards. Whoever ignores it will continue to fish blindly and, occasionally during each winter, will be amazed by strange things that happen on the ice, such as: "How could that almost dead fish pull down the rocker?" Or: "Hmm, this roach looks damaged – how can it be?" Or: "Now that little fish has fallen three times, but nothing is ever there!" And so forth.

Tackle

The basic rule in all pikeperch fishing is to tackle with as little elaboration as possible. Winter pikeperch are fastidious and can easily be disturbed by fishing tackle that is too clumsy. For this reason, one should think as if tackling "light" for perch rather than "heavy" for pike. Use relatively thin line of 0.30-0.35, and a sliding sinker of 3-8 grams that sits on the line above the leader. The leader should be of soft nylon, and a diameter of 0.50 mm is often a good compromise when fishing on pike-rich waters. If the line is otherwise 0.30-0.35 mm, the 0.50-mm leader works excellently for both pikeperch and perch, at the same time as it gives an extra margin if a pike bites.

An alternative here might be some thinner variant of the new materials, such as kevlar, which have been developed in recent years. But I have too little experience of fishing with these materials to dare make even a rough guess about how they are regarded by pikeperch. What I do know is that a steel wire, if used to angle for pikeperch, will reduce the catches to zero on many days! The leader's length should be 50-80 cm to provide a live baitfish with good mobility.

The treble hook should be no larger than No. 6, and be very sharp since the pikeperch has a hard jaw. When the fish is most sluggish, the needle-sharp hooks will result in a successfully hooked fish, while half-dull hooks invariably lead to a lost one. Not seldom, the difference between triumph and fiasco is hair-thin in pikeperch angling.

If the angling is done with large baitfish and directed toward big pikeperch, it can be justified to use hook No. 4. In addition, there are fishermen who prefer double-hook tackle of some kind. With such tackle, it may occasionally be easier to catch a pikeperch. But two great drawbacks are faced. First, the fish may spit out the bait when it is disturbed by the whole device landing in its mouth. Secondly, serious problems will arise when pike are about. This kind of tackle is soon bit off, because there are pike in most waters even when the fishing is directed toward pikeperch.

Playing the fish

Whichever type of tackle you use, it does not help the fact that pikeperch tend to be hooked half-badly or even very badly. Many come loose as soon as the strike is made, and others escape somewhere on the way up or just when being landed at the ice hole. This is equally distressing no matter when it happens. What does lie within your power is, first, to make sure that your hooks are always sharp.

Another necessity is to play the pikeperch with attention to its jerks and short rushes, so that slack line is avoided. One should also try to put a little pressure on the fish and make it relent, then take it up at an even pace. Then it can often be swept up onto the ice in a single movement. If you see that the hook sits badly, proceed slowly as the fish approaches the hole. Often it turns its belly upward and tenses its body upon contact with the ice. In this situation, a helping hand or a gaff hook will soon get the fish to land on the right side of the ice roof.

An experienced pikeperch fisherman frequently notices at an early stage whether he is dealing with a pikeperch or, for example, a pike. This can be seen especially from how the fish rushes. A lively pike makes long, quick, sweeping rushes that usually extend diagonally toward the bottom. A lively pikeperch makes shorter runs that are more like "boring" itself vertically downward, trying again and again to turn and go straight down. If it is really pugnacious, it may completely lose its bearings and lash out violently, heading in any direction at all – even up towards the ice roof!

Cunning bites by pikeperch

If you use the signal rocker of ice-fishing gear as a bite indicator when you angle for pikeperch on the winter ice, be attentive to how the rocker moves. It happens now and then that a pikeperch approaches and pulls at the baitfish without releasing the rocker. A pikeperch may even stay in this manner for several minutes with no indication. Indeed, it may swallow the bait and still give no signal!

However, the last phenomenon is quite rare. Normally the pikeperch spits out the bait after a moment, unless the fisherman acts fast and helps the indicator – by freeing the line from the feeler's top, or bending the rocker downward so that the loop slides off by itself. This may lead the pikeperch to continue its bite, though not necessarily.

Another, commoner occurrence is that the rocker actually falls in a rather typical way for pikeperch. It goes slowly and decisively down. But nothing much happens after that – the pikeperch does not pull out any line. When the fisherman comes forward, the line just points straight into the hole.

Whoever is inexperienced, or is simply used to pike fishing,

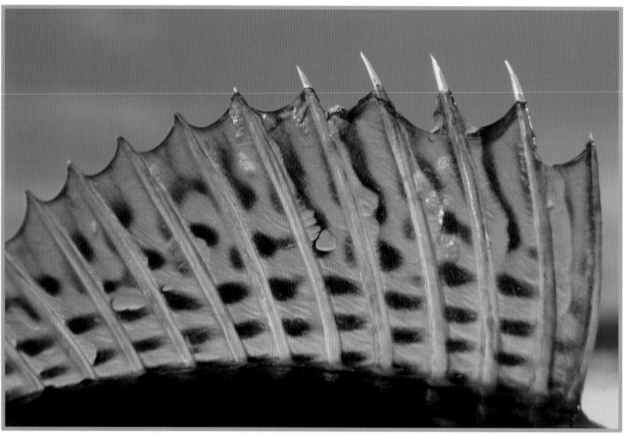

A pikeperch's dorsal fin may be beautiful, but it is not a plaything and makes an effective defence.

will then take the line and lift it a little. Next, he pulls on it a bit, and finds that nothing is there but the baitfish, so he hangs the loop back over the top of the rocker. What this fisherman has failed to notice is that a pikeperch really was there holding the bait! It held on until he first pulled the line – and then it spat out. He did not notice because of his habit in pike fishing; therefore he grabbed the line too insensitively, and provoked the pikeperch to spit immediately.

To appreciate the problem's delicate nature and what sort of sensitivity can be needed to feel that there is really a pikeperch down at the other end of the line, a fisherman ought to train the responsiveness of his fingers. Sound the water with a 0.35-mm line at ten metres of depth. On the end of this line is a 4-gram sinker, half a metre above the fish hook. You should be able to feel exactly when the little sinker lifts from the bottom. With the same concentration, you can then not only perceive but also differentiate the next source of resistance, which comes from something sitting on the hook.

Thus, in practical fishing it is a matter of cautiously feeling whether this resistance is due only to the baitfish, or whether a pikeperch is present too. If the latter, it will be slightly provoked and react in one of two ways. Either it starts to chew a little, turning the prey so that it can swallow, which causes small tugs on the line – or else it begins to move very slowly, tensing the line a bit. Then you should relax the line and give the pikeperch some time to turn the bait, making a strike after 5-30 seconds. Here one must test until one finds out what rhythm the pikeperch obeys on that day.

If one does not have this sensitivity in one's fingers, the following can be done. When the line stretches motionless into the ice hole after a bite, and little or no line has been pulled away, carefully free the line from the reel so that any fish there will feel no resistance from the reel. Ideally, feed some of the loose line down into the hole. Then wait 30-60 seconds and observe closely whether a fish seems to be pulling out line. If so, keep feeding line, and finally make a decisive strike. This

After a pikeperch bites, the fisherman often reaches the hole to find the line lying lifeless and lax, or only slightly tensed. It is then that he has to make the right moves.

If the pikeperch does nothing when you carefully tense up the line, try to provoke it a little more. Make some millimetre-sized tugs on the line, resembling a trembling. This can nudge the fish to start chewing and completing the attack.

Right: The T-tactic means starting to work in a straight line out from land or across a body of water. Once the fish are roughly found, they are located in detail by focusing on that depth or area.

entire procedure can take half a minute to two minutes, depending on how the pikeperch behaves – that is, how much time it wants for possibly turning the baitfish and stuffing the meal fully into its mouth.

Despite all the waiting, the pikeperch frequently sits well on the hook, farthest out in the jaw's tip. Still, as we have seen, whoever does not find the dance rhythm, or understand how peculiar a pikeperch can be, will miss every fish. Those who learn to dance along with the fish's slow pace will succeed well – not every time, but more often.

Tactics and searching

Something about the tactics in pikeperch angling has already been mentioned: that it is sometimes important to come out early on the fishing ice, and to stay awhile after the onset of dark. But more crucial is an understanding that all pikeperch fishing from the ice basically involves searching for the fish. One has to begin by ringing in productive areas where they are localized. On large waters, searching is a two-step procedure, and the first step is to find out which part(s) of a lake will be relevant, which bay(s) the pikeperch are in, or the like.

Here the local fishermen can often supply good tips. These may be very valuable and time-saving, as it frequently turns out that the pikeperch consist of stocks that appear in certain areas or parts of the water. Local knowledge can also inform you, for instance, that pikeperch during the current winter have been encountered in unusually great numbers within a particular cove, whereas fewer have occurred in a bay that is normally full of them. Although winter pikeperch commonly return to their favourite habitats, the latter may vary slightly from year to year, due to conditions such as wind directions that prevailed during the late autumn or when the ice formed.

The second step is to look more carefully for exact fishing places – cliffs, channels, headlands, underwater ridges, coves, sunken rocks, edges of deep holes, and so on. This is because pikeperch in the winter tend to park, not only

within certain areas, but often quite locally on rather small portions of them, and then do not stray far from these during the season. The difference is striking from summer pikeperch, which are frequently long-distance wanderers.

Fear no wide open spaces – go straight out!

When you find yourself at an interesting place and begin to search for pikeperch, a good fundamental rule is to move directly out on the water, rather than parallel to a shore. For example, if the fishing is to start at a depth of 6 metres, and 30 metres off a headland, you should not be afraid to search further at a 90-degree angle from the headland –

The T-tactic

If the first contacts with pikeperch prove to be made at 150-200 metres from shore, it is also at this distance that one proceeds to fish parallel with the shore. Presumably there will be a nearby cliff, plateau, or deep hole that the fish are frequenting. Thus one should concentrate the fishing at the same area and distance from land, as long as the depth is fairly constant. If the depth is sounded regularly while fishing, it is easy to detect any variation. The fisherman's path then takes the shape of a T, whose shaft is the searching and distancing out from shore. The cross-bar of the T shows that the search continues "horizontally" in relation to the shore.

At the fishing places you find, the subsequent task is to aim for individual pikeperch that are lingering at or near them, often together with a group of others. This can be done by moving the rods away from "inactive" spots and ringing in those where numerous contacts occur.

Small details may become significant

On snow-free ice, it can be rewarding to seek pikeperch near the joins between old grey ice and new, more translucent ice. The fish are commonly drawn to such borders between light and shadow. Similarly, patches of snow on clear ice provide shadows that can attract fish. The opposite rule is also valid: fish on snow-covered ice tend to prefer areas that let down more light. Fishing at the edges of ice channels or fairways is a classic approach, since many fish seek out these lighter areas during high winter.

How an exact search is carried out can be learned from experienced ice-fishermen. They know that, as a rule, much more time has to be spent at a newly drilled hole than in ordinary searches for perch. In addition, they know that pikeperch can be hard to coax into physical motion, so their holes are drilled closely together. Whereas a perch fisherman seldom stays longer than one or two minutes at a hole that yields no fish, a seasoned pikeperch fisherman may sit for ten minutes or more before drilling a new hole only a few metres alongside the previous one and repeating the procedure.

In sum, pikeperch – like large perch, for that matter – need more time in order to reveal that the place is right. This, how-

straight into the bay. It may very well happen that the first pikeperch contact occurs, say, 150 metres from land at 9 or 14 metres of depth. A nice bonus, too, is that the movement also teaches you a lot about the behaviour and holding places of pike.

Fishing depths of 5-15 metres

In lakes of normal to great depth, ice-angling is usually best between about 5 and 15 metres. Pikeperch that find their way into shallower water than 3 metres in this type of lake, or bay, or rare. Angling in places deeper than 20 metres will tend to bring practical problems. It takes a long time to sound the depth, sink the baitfish, and so forth.

A lovely four-leaf clover that illustrates how very different species can jointly enrich the dinner table. This time the catches were made at a free-lying sunken rock.

ever, is of little significance when the fishing method is angling, since a winter angler often uses several rods and it takes some time to rig them up.

Further, pikeperch – like pike, but even more clearly – tend to bite only during certain distinctive periods. Between these times, they bite only sporadically and, on the whole, very cautiously and hesitantly.

Pikeperch weather and biting periods

Another resemblance to pike is that, whichever way the weather changes, pikeperch respond positively. They differ radically from perch, which react negatively to a falling barometer. In other words, stable high pressure that turns to mildly low pressure, or vice versa, is usually reliable weather for catching pikeperch. Generally speaking, too, better fishing in daytime results from cloudy days and persistent

low pressure than from sunshine and continuous high pressure. The beginning of a mild weather period, after an interval of cold, normally yields good fishing. The days closest to this transition seem best.

Under the above kinds of conditions, pikeperch can often be caught all day long until dusk. But with other types of weather, you should be prepared for the fish's activity to show more limitation to one or a few periods during a fishing day. The intervening times, occasionally several hours, may exhibit no activity or interest in food at all. These dead intervals have only a single remedy – to busy yourself in searching for fish, constantly drilling new holes and presenting bait at new spots. Between the biting periods, this tactic is the sole means of getting more than a sporadic stray fish.

In other respects, the biting periods of pikeperch often coincide with those of pike and perch. This is usually quite clear and tangible. But since pikeperch are the fish they are –

with fine vision for hunting at dusk – they also have biting periods which are entirely their own. Like those of pike, the biting periods of pikeperch may vary from 10 minutes to a couple of hours in length, and they seem to approach shore when hunting in the morning or late afternoon. The difference is that, while pike may go all the way in to a shallow shore edge at 1 metre of depth, pikeperch are commonly satisfied to follow the first deep edge a little farther out in 3-6 metres of water.

In very deep lakes, the most fruitful winter angling for pikeperch is normally on medium-depth bays and in coves with 6-15 metres of water. Underwater plateaus, ridges and rocks that are surrounded by greater depths offer interesting places that must be investigated too. In shallow flatland lakes of more uniform depth, it can pay to look for pikeperch in the deepest spots, and they may also be found in the pondweed outside a reedy cove at 2.5-3 metres.

Big pikeperch and their surprises

As dedicated fishermen, we sometimes have experiences that go against the patterns we have begun to establish about a particular fishing water, a special fishing method, or the behaviour of a given species. This tends to happen just when we are feeling a little secure in the saddle. Even if the world is not thereby turned upside down, at least a new element of uncertainty enters the sport. We do not stand as routinely solid as before, and a whiff of the newcomer's wonder whirls around us.

These encounters with unexpected situations, or with fish that act strangely, yield the profit that our preparation for the unusual increases, once we have adjusted to the novelty and accepted any loss of fish that it entails. Ultimately, I think, such surprising and occasionally astonishing experiences are what make us more attentive and skilful fishermen. Hence they help us at times to hook and land fish that we would have managed only with great luck a few seasons earlier.

But however much practice, sensitivity and awareness we have collected, there is always more to learn. This is particularly true when big pikeperch are about. Every winter I myself have one or two meetings of the kind, whose outcome is highly uncertain. Sometimes I ask how many big pikeperch have passed me and never been contacted, a question that remains in the depths of the unknown.

The problem with big winter pikeperch is that they act quite unpredictably when they bite. Occasionally they are decisive and gluttonous, meaning "simple" and rewarding to deal with – at least if the playing can be managed, since big pikeperch are able to fight furiously and, when determined, worse than big pike. Yet it is not unusual for them to behave very differently. In some cases I have become completely confused by their style, and already from the first bite onward. They can prove to be utter cowards when taking the bait!

Several times, therefore, I have misjudged the bite and been convinced that it came from a really small fish, when the truth was just the contrary. As a result, I have also been amazed when the treble hook was driven in by my strike.

Meetings with big pikeperch

My first example of being taken unawares by a pikeperch occurred in late January. The place was an unfamiliar sunken rock in the middle of a large bay that I had not visited previously. The fishing had the character of sounding, and my companion Kjell and I decided to walk on each side of this rock, which was only about 10 by 20 metres large. It had a shallower side at 3-10 metres where Kjell walked, and a much deeper side at 9-20 metres where I walked. This was a typical midwinter day with stable high pressure and a few degrees below freezing. The sky was cloudy and the visibility clear. Our angling bait was live smelt of 15-18 cm.

The biting pattern had been regular during this period of protracted high pressure. Fishing in the morning was definitely best, and some days also provided a rush late in the afternoon. The same pattern applied to the short January day in question, with a fast start of biting between 8:30 and 10:00 AM.

But only Kjell's invitations got any answers – and impressive ones. Big perch were on the move! Soon he had caught three fine 1-kg specimens on the shallower part of the rock, besides a couple of pike and, presumably from perch, a number of further bites. At the same time, my deep side of the rock was completely calm for the first 45 minutes. I had nothing to do but increasingly envy Kjell's strides between four rods in action.

By 9:45, at any rate, I had landed two pike that took the bait at 10-11 metres. Meanwhile, though, Kjell was rewarded with some more excellent perch, and my envy began to suggest that I move my rods to his side of the rock. Fortunately, I did not give way to the impulse. Our original plan, in fact, was to visit the water in search of pikeperch. It had been arranged

If the water contains large pikeperch, they may appear at any moment, not seldom when you least expect them.

to investigate both the shallow and deep sides of the rock. I had to remind myself of this, once Kjell's harvest of large perch threatened to ruin most of the day's pleasure for me. And my stoicism paid off.

The last bite during this period was on my side, and came very cautiously. When the "budgie tinkler" rang from one of my rods, the time was nearly 10 AM. Having four rods to choose among, I watched intensely. It took half a minute before the rocker on the farthest rod began to dip slowly. Standing some 40 metres from the rod, I could see how the rocker sank almost imperceptibly, as when a little baby pike is biting. Finally after another half minute, the loop slipped from the well-bent rocker, which flipped up and beckoned encouragingly. However, as the bite reminded me strongly of the two pike I had caught earlier, I thought it was another pike, although much smaller. My enthusiasm was thus only moderate and I did not hurry to the rod. Kjell's fine perches

had taken the bait with far greater energy, and the presence of pikeperch at this place was something I had, as yet, no real belief in. It was not without frustration at the state of affairs that I trudged over the ice to try hooking another mini-pike.

The first thing I saw was the line loop, stuck in the ice crust that had formed in the hole. This usually means that the fish has spat out the bait. But one can never be sure, and I have developed a procedure for such situations. I tap away the crust with my forefinger and see how the line loop, with another foot or so of line, glides down through the hole. This is the amount of line that normally goes out before the sinker hits the bottom. Yet then nothing happened.

After waiting for half a minute, I began to suspect that the bite was short – the fish must have already spat when the loop got caught in the crust. Carefully I gripped the line and tensed it, centimetre by centimetre. Suddenly it began to move! When the fish had pulled out a metre of line, I made a strike

This big pikeperch of 6.3 kg did not bite properly until a little 10-cm roach was presented.

and was startled by the effect. A long tug-of-war ensued, through ice two feet thick. This big fish did not want to leave the bottom, and since I was using no leader, I did not dare to put too much pressure on it.

Eventually I could place a gaff in the tip of its jaw and pull up a pikeperch 88 centimetres long, weighing nearly 6.5 kilograms. It was an extraordinarily thin specimen with a large head – and full of parasitic worms, indicating that it had hidden passively for a considerable time on the bottom. As for why it bit at all, the only explanation can be that I happened to drill a hole and sink my smelt right in front of its nose. In other words, a stroke of pure luck.

One might think that such a big fish should not need to pull as weakly when biting as this pikeperch did. But here, too, is a rather typical way of behaving for pikeperch when they are in poor form. As a pikeperch angler, one has to realize and accept it.

Pikeperch have principles that they stick to. Nobody can lure them to swallow a baitfish when they are absolutely fasting. Nonetheless, they may bite if it is served closely enough and for long enough. With patience and a little coaxing, they can then be hooked.

Small baits

Curiously, I have caught several big pikeperch that behaved much in the above fashion. One occasion took place on a small inland lake, while fishing far inside a cove only 4 metres deep. At intervals of half an hour, I got three bites on the same rod, and each time the fish spat out. My bait consisted of medium-size roach, about 15 cm long. The problem was solved by switching to a much smaller roach of 8-9 cm. This should have been a perfect morsel for the pikeperch that was probably still down there. Assuming that it was big enough and came back, the whole bait ought to have disappeared into its jaws.

Another half hour passed before the pikeperch came back. Just as slowly as before, the rocker was drawn down. Now I knew that the bait was small, so the hooking could be done quickly. This time too, the catch was a pikeperch weighing well over 6 kg.

Thus, both of those six-kilogram specimens took rather small baits – and in a manner which led me to expect smaller quarry on the hook. The second big pikeperch had also repeatedly spat out a roach that is normally very easy for such a large one to eat. This is a good example of the fact that pikeperch of the older generation, from a sportfisherman's viewpoint, can behave at least as strangely as much younger and smaller ones do. At such times, the best tactic is seemingly to change to a smaller bait than what has previously been rejected.

It is often the case that a smaller bait need not even be live. A resolute pikeperch angler who only has access to, say, large 20-cm roaches will get plenty of interrupted bites on them. If he follows such a bite with a change to a little piece of dead fish on the hook, he should not be surprised if a pikeperch bites strongly within a short time.

Large baits

My fishing companion Kjell Appelgren frequently uses a different strategy when angling for pikeperch. He likes to fish with really large baits – roach of 100-300 grams, or smelt of

The same happened here. A slightly bigger roach was spat out twice. Only when the little roach was presented could the pikeperch be hooked well.

20-25 cm – on at least one or two rods. Not seldom, this has turned out to work well for both big pike and big pikeperch.

The disadvantage of such large baits in pikeperch angling is that a great number of pikeperch are lost during a winter. They spit out the bait, which is simply too large for the majority when they are not in good form. On the other hand, during days when their form improves, Kjell often gets the biggest specimens. Even smaller ones will then consume such large roaches.

A good instance of the superiority of large baits at the right time is the following, from an instructive day in February. I was just beginning my career as an ice-angler. Kjell had placed his row of rods in a straight line, with mine on the left and those of Björn on the right. Thus he was enclosed on both sides by our rods, or so we thought until proved wrong.

True to his habit, Kjell baited two lines with large roach, while Björn and I used more reliable prey – roach of small and medium size. But this was a day with substantial activity under the ice, and big fish were present. The consequences could be grasped by Björn and me only at the end, when we beheld the catch.

Kjell's triumph had been almost total. There was no debating it, and good reason to learn from it. On two rods with large bait, he had caught all of the day's big fish: not just fine pike, weighing up to 7.7 kg, but also a couple of 6-kg pikeperch. Moreover, nearly every pikeperch over 3 kg had bit on Kjell's two rods. The sole exception was encountered by Björn, who eventually hung out a large roach of his own. Before long, he could weigh in a 5-kg pikeperch.

For my part, I had not at all suffered during the day's fishing. With the most fish of both kinds, I was able to stand proud. But the fact remained that my fish were of merely normal size – none over 2.5 kg – and even though I had finally set up a couple of rods right next to Kjell's, to see whether the big fish were limited to that area. Still, the bites I got on my smaller baits were from the same sort as before: smaller fish. This was a day for big fish, and for Kjell, given that we were indeed looking for big fish.

To the preceding example it need only be added that, when a pikeperch is in the mood for biting, it is relatively easy to deal with as a predator. Then it opens its entire mouth and sucks in even large baits in a fraction of a second. Just a tiny puff of scales is left where a sizable roach once hung. The pikeperch swims away and can be hooked at speed with no trouble.

As we have seen, Kjell has a tactic of always using one or two rods with large baits, even on days when the pikeperch are sluggish or rather neutral in their willingness to bite. Such behaviour, of course, is unknowable in advance. On these "neutral" days, the fish may act erratically and surprise us in every way.

During a day of this kind, Kjell was fishing at one of our common niches for pikeperch. He then got a type of bite that happens now and then with invariable surprise. The large roach was baited on ice-fishing gear converted for angling. Suddenly the roach became restless, and the rocker began to rise slowly from its deeply bent position. After an interval of disturbance, it had risen so far that it stood straight up. A rocker does so only when the bait, for some reason, starts to swim upward in the water – often because it is scared by a predator which is pursuing it.

Having stood there awhile, the rocker went back to the natural position – and then it fell. But the biting fish did not pull out any line. Still more amazement awaited Kjell when he took the line in hand. It felt slack and empty, with no contact. The depth was 10 metres at the spot, and he hauled in the line to establish some contact that might reveal what was happening. Only after 8-9 metres were retrieved did the line tense up. Hence, the fish had left the bottom and risen to only a metre from the ice hole. Kjell's feet might have been just above the fish where he stood on the snow-covered ice roof.

At the same moment as Kjell made a cautious, decisive strike, the circus sprang to life. A very heavy fish pulled out all the line he had hauled in. Once the line was entirely out again, and the fish was back on the bottom, the struggle calmed down.

The tug-of-war with this veritably huge pikeperch lasted for nearly 15 minutes, before the hook came loose. During the adventure, Kjell got the fish to the hole several times, and could tell that it was a pikeperch of around 10 kilograms. I have no reason to doubt the report, as Kjell has caught some enormous pikeperch through the years, even of that size. And the same fishing place, earlier as well as later, has yielded 10-kg pikeperch.

In regard to behaviour, it was probably this big pikeperch which pursued the roach that fled up toward the ice roof. How the rocker subsequently fell, or why the pikeperch moved right up to the ice hole, can only be imagined. Perhaps it got tangled in the fishing line while chasing the roach, and knocked down the rocker as it approached the ice-fishing gear.

Similar bites, with baitfish that are pursued high up in the water, have occurred at other times. This is not an extremely unusual phenomenon, at least in connection with pikeperch. Once when the fishing was done over 8 metres of water, on thin clear ice, the pikeperch came sailing by just under the ice roof and, after a strike, was hauled home.

Winter pikeperch often stay quite calm after biting. But sometimes they take off at great speed, and can then be a match for sprinting pike. Since pikeperch and pike are commonly at odds with each other in daily temperament, I have actually guessed right on several occasions that the fish was a big pikeperch running away with the line. These were days of calm among the pike, whereas the pikeperch raced in proportion to their size – hoping to rid themselves of the irritating "appendage".

Thus, a sportfisherman is wise to be prepared for anything at all when it comes to pikeperch, especially large ones. This is what makes angling for them in wintertime a particularly uncertain and exciting sport.

Angling and chumming with dead bait

Pikeperch are perhaps the most rewarding of predatory fish to angle with dead bait. Due to their well-developed sense of smell, they have no hesitation in plucking food directly from the bottom, and it can even pay to chum from the fishing spot. Ideally, this should be done a few days before fishing, so that they have time to find the place. But if they are moving around, the chumming can yield immediate results on the same day.

Fresh baitfish that are cut in pieces and sunk right through the drilled ice hole, which can then be used as a fishing hole, may attract pikeperch to the spot surprisingly fast. And they come to eat the fish pieces – including one that serves as bait and is hung a foot over the bottom.

Perch
(Perca fluviatilis)

Perch are by far the most popular target of winter fishing. For many years my thoughts were so dominated by all the traditions and refinements of ice-fishing that no other way of catching perch seemed possible. Fishing for perch in the winter seemed to be synonymous with ice-fishing, and primarily with vertical pirks and powerful hooks. The mormyshka's entrance on stage has also meant that the development towards small baits for sluggish winter perch is winning further ground.

But parallel with this trend towards smaller baits and more sensitive equipment, an opposite tendency has been observable: continued success with the much larger balance pirk. This shows that perch, especially big ones, gladly go on with their natural hunting behaviour even after the ice is laid down. In other words, they are interested in a fish diet during the winter too. The point is that many a big perch starts to hunt the seductive balance pirk every winter precisely because of its swimming, fish-like characteristics.

Such ice-fishing with balance pirks is perhaps most successful at the beginning and end of winter, when the activity under the ice is greatest. But skilful balance-pirk fishermen manage to catch big perch throughout the winter. This is not very strange, as the staple food of big perch consists of fish and winter is no exception. The same is true of all waters where large perch occur. Little fish are the precondition for a body of water to hold big perch.

In most waters, their staple food comprises roach, bleak, smaller perch and whitefish. Among the nutrient-rich coastal archipelagos, it may be made up of equal parts of small fish and insects. Small sticklebacks, young eel, and small eel-pouts alternate with water lice, seaweed lice and shrimp – as well as herring on occasion. In smelt-bearing lakes, the food is often dominated by smelt. In lakes with plenty of crayfish, these are sometimes combined with a fish diet by large perch, supplemented by insects at intervals since a perch is interested in whatever moves.

For an ice-angler it is a great advantage to know the given water's composition of preyfish, and how richly they occur. If angling for big perch takes place in an ordinary lake, it should

Even a small roach looks big next to normal pirks.

be done with small perch. Where smelt predominate, one can take for granted that they constitute the staple diet and will therefore yield the best catches when angling. Large waters may also vary locally: for instance, angling with smelt can be outstanding at considerable depths, while roach bait can be quite good around shallower spots and along reed banks.

If one looks at the format and size of the pirks that are used to find perch in winter, they are generally rather small – particularly in comparison with the live fish that may be used as baits in ice-angling. When ice-angling with live baitfish, we must be content with the bait sizes we happen upon, which are much larger and "clumsier" than the elegant, beautiful balance pirks of fry size that the trade supplies.

A roach of 10-14 cm is obviously gigantic in relation to a normal balance pirk. Even so, the fishing is usually better with baitfish of such a size than with much smaller baitfish. How can this be explained? Probably by the fact that a perch would attack a smaller, or young, baitfish if the latter were presented.

But winter fishing involves searching, and a little baitfish cannot take being moved from hole to hole as large ones can; besides, a larger baitfish makes more noise and attracts predators more strongly. As a result, more big pike are drawn to large baitfish in the winter. Things might be different if we had the possibility of sinking a small fry when the perch have started to move and are where we want them – namely, beneath the hole we are fishing in.

Trying to tempt perch with the relatively large bait that I recommend will offer an additional advantage: roach and live smelt, respectively 10-14 and 14-18 centimetres long, separate out the small perch. Then the fishing is concentrated on the examples that concern us: perch weighing from nearly a pound upward. These perch are impressive hunters and normally have no problem with gorging on roach and smelt of the above size – at least not as long as they are alert and eager to hunt. Then the smelt are pushed in from all directions, indeed with double weight.

However, on really sluggish days, it may happen that only the true heavyweights will bother to bite. I remember a late, very cloudy January day on a bay, when the barometer fell sharply. The fishing took place at 8 metres of depth and the perch were very sluggish. One had to bring the hook, baited with a little roach, right in front of their noses. In this way I eventually succeeded – though it took until just after sunset – in coaxing up three big perch, all exceeding the kilogram mark. Smaller perch paid no attention at all to roaches on this day. Presumably I was also helped by the tactical finesse of finally changing down to the smallest roaches I could find in my baitfish bucket. These roaches were only a couple of centimetres shorter than those I had previously tempted the perch with. But it was evidently enough to keep the big perch from breaking off their cautious bites as they had done earlier in the day. When a perch is sluggish, all its activities are governed by the law of least resistance!

In general, big perch are known for taking their time before biting. Only accustomed ice-fishermen for perch, who are not averse to sitting a little longer at every hole, regularly have the pleasure of coming to grips with big perch in winter. Those who are adapted to the techniques of competition ice-fishing, with fast shifts to new holes and places, do not get to feel such heavy pulls very often during a winter. One or two minutes at an ice hole are seldom enough to attract the predator in a recently awakened big perch. Here the ice-angler has time to spare. Since we use several rods, the fishing has a natural rhythm of not moving about too fast. Thus the big perch are given the time they need. And once the first of them swallows our live bait, we can usually entice more of the same sort, if we are sufficiently quick to unhook and to sink a new baitfish.

The perch's activity in wintertime

In terms of the winter as a whole, perch are by no means as active and liberal in their consumption or search for food as during the summer. Reduced energy expenditure and metabolism in the winter cold decrease their need for food dramatically. They eat only for short periods, mainly in the daytime.

However, perch are least active in the water of freezing temperature when ice is forming. Then they can usually be found on deep bottoms where the water is a little warmer and less turbulent. After a week or so of new ice, as the earth's warmth raises the water temperature, the perch become ever more active and mobile over greater areas. It is not uncommon to find large hunting groups of big perch along coastal reed beds during early morning and towards evening.

In midwinter, big perch tend to stay at greater depths. Thus, many perch fishermen make the mistake of continuing to seek them near shore, and on the shallow sunken rocks where they were caught successfully earlier in the winter.

As late winter approaches, the perch begin a more definite migration back from the depths toward the shores. This occurs in step with the spring sun as its warm rays start to penetrate through the ice. When the spring meltwater reaches the bottom, flies begin to hatch and the groundwater is increasingly populated.

During this time, freshly hatched flies rise from the bottom toward the ice roof. Frequently, old ice-fishing holes and cracks in the ice are full of empty nymph cases. Up on the ice, the hatched flies crawl around – that is, the ones which have survived. For the small fish have also noticed what is happening, and take the insects in all water layers, even the highest. It is now that the perch seriously approach shore and swim up on the shallow pondweed rocks, hunting both flies and small fish. This is a golden chance for balance-pirk ice-fishermen, and for anglers!

Perch and the formation of ice

What takes place in the water during ice formation is very important for how the fishing will be in the next weeks. Paying some attention to weather and wind around this time can provide hints on how the perch fishing should be organized in the introductory stage of winter fishing.

The ice can be bound by water in different ways. Most favourable is a combination of strong cold with absence of wind. Then the surface water is cooled rapidly and the ice begins to form immediately. Perch that have previously wandered out onto deep bottoms will now stay there, since the water temperature is best in the depths. Heat radiation from the bottom there is sufficient to maintain a uniform, optimal temperature of about 4°C (40°F). These perch which are left on the deep bottoms become acclimatized fairly soon to the low, uniform temperatures, and can rather easily be attracted to bite even on the first ice.

By contrast, if the ice formation takes much time and is preceded by storms, with air temperatures that vary around or

Many perch lakes regularly offer superior winter fishing on the first new ice.

below freezing, then the water temperature drops in shallow lakes at all water levels, so low that the perch go into hibernation. Due to the stiff cold, they become almost incapable of moving, and perch fishing is virtually useless. Several weeks may then pass before the earth's warmth raises the bottom temperature so that life among the luscious becomes more normal. Meanwhile, burbot and pike, which tolerate cold better, will have exploited the opportunity to feast on these easy prey.

But the perch fishing need not be pointless even during this difficult period. There may be exceptional localities in a lake that is covered with ice in such a way. What should be sought are the deeper lee coves where hard wind has not set the water in motion. Here the temperatures are kinder and the chances of luring perch are best. It can also be worth knowing which part of the lake was first to become ice-covered. In this area the perch awaken and start moving sooner after the cold shock.

In deeper lakes with such ice formation, the effect of pervasive cooling the water may be different. It is not certain that the entire water mass has time to be cooled throughout. Thus at times, in spite of extreme cooling, one can find concentrations of active perch in various middle layers where pockets of water with higher temperature have formed.

Equipment and tactics

In perch angling, we can take advantage of the same tackle as is used in angling for pikeperch.

This equipment can cope with most pike as well. But if the fishing is adjusted for big perch alone, thin lines of around 0.20 mm diameter can naturally be used. It is definitely helpful if you have been lucky enough to obtain fry bait.

When the perch are in good form, they swallow more

When fishing for perch, one can often see that the roach is very chafed on its neck and sides, but that it lacks the wounds characteristic of attacks by pike and pikeperch, or the bloodshed that usually occurs when these toothy predators have been on the scene.

rapidly than either pike or pikeperch. Then even a double weight of roach or smelt can be taken in, and they try to swallow it immediately. The whole process may be over in 5-10 seconds. Occasionally a perch is also just as fast to spit, so the fisherman should be on the spot and make a strike before the fish has regrets and quickly blows the bait out of its jaws.

When the perch are sluggish, they take a lot of time. One is then reminded more strongly of pikeperch, except that perch seldom bite without serious intentions. If only given enough time, a perch will usually turn the bait right in its mouth and start to swallow. It then takes the line at a calm tempo and you can often make the strike immediately. If the bait is large or the perch is not very big, it may need a couple of minutes before the strike.

Frequently a perch takes more line in the initial stage than a pike or pikeperch would, as these tend to stay at the scene of the crime for a while before moving away.

Playing the fish

The winter's big female perch, as a rule, are so fat and full of roe that they cannot attain much speed. But they can still pull the line hard! There is scarcely any risk of their breaking a leader, since they lack teeth. However, one must keep in mind that a perch's jaw has no fleshy elasticity as in many other fish. If a perch is hooked solidly in the hard, sensitive outer part of the mouth, a risk always exists that the thin skin may break if the fish is taken too strongly and, at the same time, is shaking to get loose. Once the hole where the hook sits is destroyed, the hook easily slides out again.

Farther inside the perch's jaw, too, the hook often fastens only moderately well. To prevent a big perch from being lost needlessly, it should therefore not be taken too hard. And once it is about to be brought up onto the ice, this is done most securely with the help of a small sharp gaff, or else by hand. The small gaff – a large sharpened treble hook, firmly lashed to a stick – easily gets a "grip" in the perch even when not penetrating. With this grip, the perch slides smoothly up through the hole, being pressed against the ice edge. When fishing in the manner of catch-and-release, the perch can later be returned to the water despite having been taken by "gaff".

Where the perch are

The perch is a typical warm-water lover. It constantly seeks out the warmest water in winter, which is just over the bottom at 4°C (40°F). This temperature does lie far from the perch's optimal temperature, which is thought to be around 18°C (65°F), but nothing warmer can be found during the winter.

In other respects, the perch is largely governed by the principle that seems to control all live – maximum possible calorie intake and least possible calorie loss. During wintertime, this may mean for example that the perch prefers to stay at a place where it does not have to suffer a needless loss of calories on a task such as parrying currents of water – it looks for calm water. Currents often occur in large, elongated lakes, for instance when rain falls over part of the lake. The increased pressure on the water pushes it in one direction or another, resulting in currents, sometimes so strong that the perch move to the lee behind a headland and wait to take food that may be carried past.

The basic tip for finding big winter perch in midwinter, though, is due to the perch's attitude toward the barometer. When the air pressure is even and stable, it is found on flat bottoms. If the barometer rises, it is sought on sloping or smooth bottoms. With falling air pressure, it is fished on sloping bottoms and ideally at depth in a direction toward the shallows.

Throughout the period of ice, when there is much snow, one can also succeed by fishing in slush patches and next to cracks, which let down a little extra light into the dark beneath the covered surface. The same applies to open stretches, and even a small area ploughed clear of snow will let down so much light that both small fish and predators are attracted. On smooth ice, the opposite advice holds – to fish near accumulations and patches of snow that can give the fish shade and cover. Here they gladly stand in the joins between shady and open, unprotected waters.

Topography for perch

As for other features of topography, there is a wide variation in the locations of perch in different lakes. One perch lake is seldom like the next. In one, we constantly find large smelt-perch out on smooth bottoms at 10-20 metres of depth. In another, the surest spots for perch are some sunken rocks at scattered points. In a third, it is a ridge stretching across a bay that continually offers perch. In a fourth, certain special headlands or coves are most rewarding. In a medium-deep (5-10 metres) and well-protected archipelago bay, particular sunken rocks may be what often attract big perch, or the fast-sloping cliffs off a mountainside. There may also be a deep rock in the middle of a bay with plenty of perch, and so on.

Seek systematically

One of the most important tactical tasks for fishing today is to discover the depth that the perch seem to like on the day in question. This may vary from day to day, not least because of barometric changes. Searching for the perch's daily depth is thus somewhat like the method recommended for seeking pikeperch. To move out from land, and then follow some systematic procedure, is preferable when looking for perch as well. For instance, decide on a line and drill a new hole every fifth to fifteenth metre. If you get a bite in the hole at a water depth of 7 metres, drill new holes sideways at that depth until no more bites are obtained.

Look for places, not fish!

Having some kind of system in your search is even more crucial when you are on unknown waters. In this case no local knowledge will be available about the depth conditions, sunken rocks, ridges, cliffs and the like. Nothing indicates which spots are usually most reliable and rewarding for fish. If no sea chart is at hand either, it soon becomes obvious that work has to be done. However, with a sea chart and a few ideas and facts about perch, hope springs eternal and a plan can be made.

What the perch fisherman must do first is to focus on finding interesting places to fish, rather than looking for fish. Since the perch normally go deep in winter, one concentrates on depths between about 5 and 12 metres. Moreover, the perch prefer hard clay bottoms – though even more clearly, clean stone bottoms! – instead of soft sedimented bottoms during the winter. In addition, we know that sunken rocks with their tops at 5-12 metres of depth, bordering still deeper water, are among the perch's favourite places in winter.

Meetings with local fishermen can yield tips on certain fishing spots or rocks that are well-reputed in a lake or bay. Yet these places are usually best at the beginning of the season.

It pays to look for perch even out on wide open spaces.

They are visited by many fishermen every weekend and soon emptied of their best stocks. Once most of the fish are taken up from them, not much attraction is left there. Thus, other possible spots should be looked for, perhaps hitherto unnoticed ones, but at least places which are visited less often.

A sea chart will help in finding untried sunken rocks, cliffs, plateaus, ridges, headlands and so forth. At a sunken rock, the main problem can be to locate its top. Once localized, it should be mapped to get an idea of both its extent, its highest point, and its other features. The top is normally the best fishing spot if there are 5-12 metres of water above it. Later in the winter, perch gladly rise to still shallower tops at 3-6 metres below the ice cover. If there are no perch around the rock's top, one should instead look for plateaus at the sides and along the rock's extended ridges in deeper water. At worst, the given rock may prove to be an unproductive one, but the next rock could be much better. A search that can take a few setbacks is usually rewarded in the end!

Perch weather and biting periods

Perch are very sensitive to variations in air pressure. They react positively with more alertness and activity when the barometer rises. Then they are relatively greedy and easy to catch. But decreasing air pressure gives them the "bends" with ever more indolence. In certain environments they are able to balance the lower pressure by swimming into deeper water. When on flat bottoms, though, they do not have this option and become out of sorts, forced to wait until their bodies adapt in swim-bladder pressure to the surrounding water pressure. After about a day, they have grown used to the prevailing air pressure and normalized their activity. In general, perch go shallower with higher pressure and deeper with low pressure.

It is interesting that a falling barometer does not always mean less eager perch. The same event can instead start the perch moving beneath the ice. This is because lower air pressure often brings precipitation in wintertime. When the snow falls on the ice and weighs it down, the water pressure increases under the ice, affecting the perch's activity just as a rising barometer does. Similarly, this explains why strong precipita-

A fisherman who holds out despite some disappointment often reaps riches.

tion during cloudy low-pressure days can speed up the perch. Moreover, the effect is identical on the majority of fish under the ice. In other words, the winter's best fishing may well take place on a day of bad weather.

Biting periods

Perch get tired quickly during the winter. Adept and experienced ice-fishermen say that the perch are exhausted after about 20 minutes of activity. This interval enables them to bring up a fair quantity of fish, but then the yield stops unless new perch arrive to continue the rush of bites.

When ice-angling, we cannot work as rapidly and smoothly as a traditional ice-fisherman. Hence there is always a risk of losing contact with the perch prematurely. While we loosen our hooks, sound the depth again, pull up the line once more, put on a new roach or smelt, and lower it into the depths, the perch in their eagerness to hunt may have time to swim away. This is an unavoidable handicap – unless we "cheat" and take out an ordinary ice-fishing rod that is kept ready. Thus, 8-10 big perch from the same hole must be considered a good result during a biting rush, if they are taken solely by angling.

After a hectic rush, the pike becomes totally uninterested for a long interval until the next biting period starts. In my own experience of ice-angling, though, the perch's biting periods are not as regular as those of pike and pikeperch. I do not know why this is the case. Sometimes the perch begin to move early in the morning, but do nothing for the rest of the day.

Nonetheless, if one is at a place where big perch are relatively scarce, it is possible to catch perch sporadically all day long until dusk. Still, the important point is that perch angling, to a higher degree than angling for pike or pikeperch, depends on active searching by the angler in order to succeed. If one can only find the perch, the angling works in the same way as ice-fishing: the mere presence of attractive food can bring a whole school of perch. Therefore, my overall impression from experience of these three species is that winter perch are easier to influ-

The perch has its own biting periods, but they often coincide with those of the pike and pikeperch.

ence than pike or pikeperch. While the latter predators hold more strictly to distinctive biting periods, the perch can be better motivated to bite in periods created by the fisherman. Success then builds largely on the fisherman's efforts – the more holes, the greater the chance of getting a group to bite.

At the end of a fishing day, it is worth returning to an area or even a hole that has proved rewarding in the morning. Any remaining perch there may very well be ready for a new confrontation.

The average weight of winter perch that are angled in the ways described above is between 0.5 and 1 kilogram. But perch that reach a kilogram are not uncommon.

Salmonoids

The salmonoids differ little from other predatory fish in regard to their fish diet. Even cultivated rainbow trout that occur in put-and-take waters react like predators at the sight of small fish.

Gluttons with poor memories

Once with my fishing comrade Kjell Appelgren, during a day in late February, I found myself on grey and snow-free ice over a sunken rock. The rock had the character of a smooth, hump-like rise with a top at 9 metres of water depth, surrounded by depths to 20 metres. We had never visited it before and did not know what awaited us, but our main hope was to catch pikeperch.

For a change, our expectations were fulfilled surprisingly fast. The first pikeperch met its fate before an hour had passed. It was followed by several more and, since also perch,

pike and even burbot were on the bite, we had collected a beautiful cloverleaf already by lunchtime.

Then Kjell innocently sank a fairly large roach over the cliff towards the depths. Suddenly the line was pulled out of his hands by a strong bite just under the ice roof. The roach had managed to descend 1-2 metres when the pull came. As the fish rushed away with the line at speed, Kjell caught it and let the run proceed for another 20 seconds. He made a stop and hooked the fish, which continued to draw out line.

The weight, strength and speed of this fish made Kjell draw my attention. He needed a gaff and, after 15 minutes of struggling, we got the first glimpse of a shiny fat salmon, swishing past the hole. In the next ten minutes, we had the fish lying crosswise under the hole three times. Personally I felt unsure whether it was really a salmon and not a sea trout, but Kjell's

---

Below: The author with a rainbow trout taken by ice-angling with a roach.

certainty persuaded me. Unfortunately, I could not lever the salmon backward far enough on any of these occasions to place the gaff properly in its lower jaw. During these efforts, it made a final rush and the hook came loose.

Since then, no further contacts with salmon have been made. But this may be primarily because we have not yet directed the fishing in their direction. In any case, I am quite confident that the potential of ice-angling also includes these highly aggressive, rapidly growing predatory fish. Salmonoids have an essentially gluttonous mentality, which prevails regardless of whether they are cultivated or wild. Moreover, they have a tendency to return time and again, at fairly short intervals, if they fail at the first bite. Thus, they are often simpler to fish than both perch and pike. The latter species seem

to have better memories and greater respect for danger.

Short memories and greediness also apply to the species in put-and-take lakes. While pike fishing for purposes of conservation, I had an opportunity to try ice-angling with live bait-fish in a small lake. The fishing was done mainly near the bottom in shallow waters at 1-5 metres. This was at the end of March, and my host explained that I should not expect a fine catch, as the lake had been open for active ice-fishing throughout the long winter and many fish were taken up without equivalent replenishment. In spite of that, the rainbow trout proved to bite eagerly – not only on my small roaches, rigged deceptively with a little treble hook in the back, but also on big roaches that were baited on a traditional hook for pike. These rainbow returned repeatedly, even

Rainbow, brook trout, and converted ice-fishing gear.

This grayling spit out a lot of fish fry when it came up on the ice.

when the roach was pulled out of their mouths by unsuccessful strikes.

In addition to rainbow and brown trout, the lake also held a very small strain of wild brook trout. Naturally, I had no hope of being able to lure them during this experimental fishing. It was thus not without surprise and some pride that I eventually lifted a wild, struggling specimen of this colourful, rare fish onto the ice. Weighing 550 grams, it had swallowed a round-bellied roach 14 centimetres long.

The experimentation also taught me that fish can be a bit fickle due to their eager biting. They not only pull in small fish quickly, but can spit out just as fast. The baitfish usually look "scrubbed", sometimes also with a "scratchiness" due to the fact that these fish, unlike perch, have tiny teeth. The tactic for regular success, therefore, should be to hook the fish almost immediately while it is in a good mood – at least if the baitfish is not very big. For the same reason, not too many rods should be spread over too large an area.

For an experimentally minded fisherman with an interest in salmonoids, many discoveries should be waiting here, since winter angling with live bait is still relatively unexplored territory. For instance, it can be worth trying for large grayling, if one has access to small bait and to good grayling waters.

Sea trout

Also comparatively easy to fish should be sea trout, if the right spots are found. With a number of rods out, the tactics of trolling can then be tried when it comes to the presentation – offering baitfish at different depths. Herring and smelt that are presented in diverse water levels, over various medium depths and so on, serve very well. But lacking these baits, even live roach seem to be accepted with little hesitation.

Baits and bait-catching

Winter ice-angling stands and falls with the possibilities of obtaining bait. Countless fishing tours have gone awry and been postponed due to lack of bait. Far from all fishermen, of course, are able to rely on the supplies that large towns and cities often provide, with the chance of buying live bait in some local sportfishing shop. But not even there can one be entirely certain of the stocks. It is thus likely that a winter fisherman sooner or later will get into a situation where bait is scarce just when needed most.

Solutions to the problem, luckily, are often available. A good way of ensuring continuous access to bait during the winter is, already in the autumn, to plan and arrange corves that are successively filled with fresh, undamaged bait before the ice is laid down. These provide solid starting capital once the season begins.

Doomed to failure, on the other hand, are attempts to corf fish as early as summertime, in the belief that they will survive until winter. In warm summer water, bacteria will multiply. The slightest damage to the fish's slime layer develops quickly into a serious bacterial or fungal infection. Only when the water has cooled down to at most 10°C (50°F) does it pay to start long-term storage. In mid-northerly countries, October is usually a suitable month in which to begin corfing.

Live or dead bait

The ideal bait for ice-angling is live. Shorter times between bites will result from more lively and fresh bait on the hook. This is the basic rule in all angling. However, it does not exclude all angling with dead bait – on the contrary. Many adept anglers even maintain that angling with dead bait is superior to angling with live bait!

So an ice-angler who, for ethical or legal or practical reasons, cannot use live baitfish is justified in feeling calm and certain that he will catch fish with dead bait instead. The main point is to make sure that the bait is fresh and no rotting process has started. Then it is by no means uncommon that both pike, pikeperch, and burbot will gladly accept such "easy-to-

Bait bucket with visible baitfish seen from above

catch" bait. Neither do perch and game fish in a hungry mood tend to refuse dead bait.

Traditional ice-fishing is often done with dead bait. If pike are moving about and hunting actively, they find their way to dead bait surprisingly soon. For a desperate fisherman, it can even be worth visiting a food store and buying some dead whole and fresh herring. Although herring belong to the sea, angling for pike with this strongly scented bait is often excellent in inland lakes too. In fact, I am not sure that whole herring are always better than cleaned herring. My fishing companions have reported that test-fishing in lakes with cleaned herring – after removal of the fins, head and guts – has succeeded well in angling for pike. Mackerel also have a strong scent and can be rewarding as bait.

When it comes to the pikeperch's attitude toward dead bait, my experience is more limited. But I had an interesting, thought-provoking experience during a February day on a bay. The ice-angling was being done with live fresh-caught smelt, the best possible bait for attracting pikeperch and perch. On one occasion, we had missed changing the water in one of the buckets holding the smelt. By the time our mistake was noticed, several smelt had died.

My companion Kjell then had a bright idea and, dividing these smelt into pieces, dropped a couple of fistfuls into two of the nearest active holes. Later, at home from the fishing tour, he dissected the stomach contents of the two pikeperch that had been caught in these "chummed" holes. Both of the 2-kilogram fish had several of the cut-up smelt pieces inside. This indicates not only that the pikeperch had a good sense of smell, but also that, when in good humour, they willingly pick up food from the bottom. Evidently they had followed the scent trail and, after finding some pieces, gone after the live smelt on the hooks that sealed their fate.

Live bait that have become almost lifeless will sometimes also attract bites. But for more regular and frequent success, the main rule still applies – alert and lively baitfish are normally superior to dead bait.

Pike, pikeperch and burbot are happy to take fresh fish pieces directly from the bottom – including a piece that is baited with a hook.

The live bait

Through the years I have had reason to try diverse kinds of live baitfish for ice-angling: bream, crucian carp, rudd, roach, perch and smelt. Since my catches have been good on all kinds, it is easy to conclude that almost anything works. At least the pike would doubtless agree with this.

In regard to pikeperch, though, my experiences differ. While roach also serve very well, it seems that pikeperch usually find smelt faster. Small crucian carp and small white bream have been rewarding, too. Yet these high-backed fish must be small if a pikeperch, which has comparatively small jaws, is to get them into its mouth without any problem.

Large-grown winter perch have an absolute, indubitable favourite, namely smelt. But in lakes and archipelagos where few smelt occur, the right bait is small roach, around 10-13 cm long. A few devoted perch anglers who are used to going after perch with bleak in the summer may not agree that such substantial roaches are ideal bait for perch with an average weight around 0.5 kilograms. What, then, of the claim that a corresponding ideal size of smelt is 15-18 cm? For this is the size that gives the most bites.

If bleak could only be found during the winter too, they would naturally get a front seat for catching perch. But I am not sure that they would be more successful. The fact is that winter and summer perch differ in behaviour. Summer perch are more active and mobile. Besides, an alert summer bleak is far better at "searching" a large area, compared to a bleak whose radius of movement is limited by a hole in the ice. As a winter bait for perch, in my opinion, bleak – as well as small roaches and smelt – become more effective only when one has gathered and got some speed into a group of winter perch. Then the bleak are an easily swallowed prey.

For those who are accustomed to traditional ice-fishing for perch, and know which small baits are best to try with, it must sound crazy to serve these big baits. Still, there are two explanations for why the larger bait sizes that I recommend are often found to be so good. One is that roaches and smelt of

Pike do not turn down any prey, but when high-backed species such as white bream (here a roach) are used to attract pikeperch and perch, they should be small in order to fit into such a fish's relatively small mouth.

The size of the bait that we use determines the lower weight limit of our catch. This 350-gram perch swallowed as much as it could.

these sizes are able to swim around and "school" in the water for hours without tiring. The other is that they send out, in all ways, stronger and clearer attractive signals to distant predatory fish than do smaller baits. Once the perch have been drawn to the spot, the bait's size really does not matter so much, as long as it is not too big for the perch to swallow.

Furthermore, smelt are a soft and pliable prey. Not seldom, even big smelt lie folded double in a perch's jaws when it is pulled up through the ice hole. An additional point is that the large size of the bait, apart from being perfect for pike and pikeperch as well, effectively sorts out the perch that weigh less than 300 grams. Thus no bait is wasted on small predators which, in any case, are rather uninteresting.

In conclusion, all kinds of fish are worth trying as bait, including dead ones. But there are two superior all-round baits that can normally be used for every predator, including sea trout and burbot, on the majority of occasions: live roach and smelt of sizes 10-14 and 15-18 centimetres, respectively.

Crucian carp versus smelt

As an ice-angler, one soon learns to appreciate the good qualities of the different fish species that may be considered as bait. For instance, crucian carp are incredibly robust and tolerant of all the strain that is put on them. They can stay in a corf as long as you like, consume minimal oxygen in a bait bucket, have a strong constitution and amazing energy as bait, and can be reused several times without tiring if you run short of bait.

Smelt have the main advantages that they are so appreciated by most predatory fish, and that they work very intensively as bait. On the other hand, they are much more fragile than other baitfish during the winter. No fish is more sensitive to staying in a bait bucket. Oxygen-poor water (change it often!), little space (do not put too many in the same bucket!), and strong cold outside (change the water often!) are factors that must be particularly heeded with smelt. But if one learns to take account of these special demands for oxygen, space, and generally careful handling, it is indeed possible to preserve even smelt for 7-8 weeks of the winter half-year.

Buying versus catching bait

There are only two fairly reliable ways for the winter fisherman to obtain his own bait. Either he resolves to buy it and hope for good, cheap supplies, or else he arranges some other way. The latter usually means catching and preserving his own bait.

Buying bait at the local sportfishing shop is quite traditional. If you only go fishing occasionally during a whole winter, this is presumably the best solution. But a different procedure is often possible for anglers who want bait for catching pike. The requirements are a little ice-fishing rod and a nearby body of water with a reasonable stock of small perch. Then a series of perch can be pulled up and preserved in a small bucket of water. Pike love them!

Catching prey with cages

If you want to be sure of a constant supply of bait in good condition, and a wide choice of suitable bait sizes, it can be a good idea to invest in a roach-hut and catch your own winter bait.

A roach-hut provides a safe, comfortable and time-saving method of catching bait. If put in the right place, it will certainly take care of your "fishing" with triumph. Left overnight or for a day and night or two, it stands always ready to admit visitors that, sooner or later, are attracted by the irresistible scent of food. Roaches, white and small bream, and crucian carp can easily be lured in.

An appropriate depth for a roach-hut is 1-15 metres. It may lie along a coastal edge or reed bed, far inside a cove or off a headland, in a channel or off a boat club's pier, in the middle of a small lake or at its outlet or inlet. Once such a place is located, one can soon bait the cage and sink it a couple of days before the planned fishing tour.

Working with two huts to catch bait can be beneficial. One of them might be placed rather shallowly near shore, for example outside reeds, and the other in deeper water farther out. During periods of mild weather, the "shallow" hut will

Långberg's classic yarn hut is a classic that still lasts.

yield more fish, while in cold periods the "deep" hut will do so as the fish migrate out to deeper water.

If a roach-house is sunk down from the ice, a sizable ice hole is needed. Creating the hole may take some effort if the ice is very thick, especially if you use an axe instead of an adequate ice pick or drill. Afterwards, it is always wise to mark the hole in some manner. This is done for two important reasons: so that nobody unwittingly steps into the hole, and so that you can find the hole even after a heavy snowstorm. The hole is subsequently covered, for example with sackcloth or a couple of pine branches. A layer of snow over this gives still better insulation.

Empty the hut often

A roach-hut should not stand out too long before being emptied. When the trapped fish have eaten to their satisfaction, or when the chum has run out, the fish try to find a way out of the cage. Small roaches – perfect for perch – disappear first. Since no further fish enter once the chum is eaten, only a small group of big fish is left after a few days. Thus, setting out the hut and letting it stand for a week before being emptied is a risky strategy. Better is to leave it for at most a couple of days and nights, then check the result. If this is scanty, it can be moved to another place; if satisfying, it can be closed.

Huts for sale

Most types of roach-huts work adequately. But there are simple, easily handled models just as there are large, clumsy ones. You can also choose between more robust types, knotted of nylon with a steady steel skeleton, and more fragile yarn huts. In addition, it is quite feasible to make your own hut from chicken-wire. Galvanized, half-hardened net is the best.

Different models vary in their ability to catch roach. But a home-made hut of cheap, galvanized chicken-wire, if properly constructed, can work very well.

Chumming

The first time your hut is sunk into the water, or after a long stay down there, you can chum abundantly both inside and outside the hut. Once the fish have grown used to the feeding place, less chumming is needed for good results.

If you delay your catch of bait until the ice has sealed the water, certain preparations can still be made. Already during the autumn, by chumming at some spots two or three metres deep, it is possible to accustom the baitfish to the place and gather roaches in those areas before winter. If this has not been done, the first results from the ice may be rather slender. But they usually improve as the chum from the hut spreads in the water.

Old half-dry light plain bread, bread rolls, boiled rice, mashed and cooked macaroni, boiled leftover portions of porridge and so on, can be well worth chumming the hut with. But even better results are obtained by also investing in scents! Roaches are attracted, for instance, by sweet aromatic substances such as honey and syrup. Aniseed, with its intense

sweet scent, is good to crush and strew in the chum blend. Coriander and fennel are classic examples of other bread spices that are often mentioned in this connection.

Old biscuits and cakes, too, are effective. I have an acquaintance in the restaurant business who even chums with old pastries, pie slices and the like – with excellent results.

Personally I am content to use about half a litre of porridge oats that have been seasoned with a little aniseed or honey. The mixture is kneaded together with nearly half a pint of water in a plastic bag. When the "dough" is fairly hard and not too sticky, it is ready to use. This oat dough does not dissolve at first. If you want a softer or drier dough that dissolves more easily and spreads its scent faster, you need only increase or decrease the amount of water. The fish are lured into the hut sooner if you smear a little of the "porridge" around its entrances.

A classic recipe is to hard-boil porridge and mix in a little linseed to improve its durability.

Aromatic extracts

Due to the development of modern angling, there are now quite a few interesting aromatic extracts to buy and flavour the chum with. Extracts are sold in both powdered and liquid forms by well-stocked fishing-equipment dealers.

Anglers usually blend the extract in crumb flour. Together with some water, the blend is baked into balls that are thrown out in the water, where they immediately dissolve and quickly attract fish to the spot.

But in order to make well-scented crumb-flour balls work with long-time effectiveness in a roach-hut, one must be a bit clever. By freezing in the water-baked balls, you can greatly lengthen their lifetime in the cold winter water, up to a couple of days and nights depending on the balls' size. The longest survival of rough treatment by the fish is ensured if these irresistible balls are first placed in a fine-meshed little net bag.

Opposite top:
Modern angling provides this assortment: frozen balls of bread crumb flavoured with a little aromatic extract.

Bottom:
Hoarding bait can begin already in late autumn, just before the first ice cover.

Preservation of baitfish

For my part, I nowadays catch most of the winter's bait already in October and early November – that is, before the ice is laid. This is a measure for sheer comfort. I have found it to be a strategy that suits me better than having to stay on the ice later on while laying and checking roach-huts. In October and November the waterways cool down rapidly, but since the water is still open, it is also easier to deal with the actual corfing, which means sorting and preserving the baitfish.

It might be assumed that such early corfing of bait, to be fished with throughout a long winter, leads to extreme decline in the condition of these fish. Almost two months pass before the first baits come into use at all. But the fact is that this presents no special problem, as long as the corfing is managed correctly. Every spring, therefore, I am able to release the fish that were never used in the winter. The net loss of individuals due to physical damage during this extensive preservation is minimal – only occasional ones per 100 specimens. Crucian carp and small roaches have proved to be most durable. Now and then in the course of their preservation, the fish can be fed with some porridge oats or bread.

Corves for long-time preservation

The long preservation of baitfish is naturally best done in nature's own care. However, if the opportunity exists, one can also do as I have seen fortunate examples of: preserving the baitfish in large containers inside a cold garage. Here, though, arrangements are required with aquarium accessories that ensure effective oxygenation and purification of the water. Smelt can also be preserved in this way. As for bait that have been caught in a roach-hut, it may be wise to leave them in a natural corf for a week before being placed in the cold garage's containers. Then they have time to get rid of all stomach contents and empty their intestines of water-polluting excrement.

A washing-machine drum made of stainless steel has become something of a classic for natural corfing of baitfish. It is tough and very "friendly" to the fish, since it lacks blunt projections that can damage the specimens preserved in it.

Both large and small plastic containers can be used as corves for winter preservation of baitfish.

Plastic corves

If you take account of the fact that a fish placed in a corf should not be exposed to the risk of scraping against rough areas of any size, then different types of plastic container are superb to use for both short- and long-time preservation. All types with a lid, including used and clean-washed paint buckets, are very easy to refashion as well-working corves. Such a container holding 10-15 litres can lodge 50-100 small roaches (of length 10-14 cm) during an entire winter. A 25-litre plastic can, with a cut-out lockable lid, can hold around 150 roaches of the same size.

Bigger baits in large quantities call for more roomy containers in order to cope with a long time in corves.

For these plastic corves to function, the same principle is followed by them all. It is very important that the preserved fish have good access to oxygen. This is ensured by peppering a plastic corf with drill holes of size 5-8 mm, at intervals of about 5 cm. Also drill some holes in the lid – but not in the bottom of the container, if it is to be stored standing on its bottom. Otherwise the container will fill with sludge. When the holes are drilled, small hard projecting plastic "screws" will form on the insides of the container, and must be removed to prevent damage of the fish.

With a large enough, non-blunt weight in the bottom, and with a string tied on the top, such "corves" will hang straight and stand upright. But all this effort will be to no avail if the storage place itself is poor in oxygen! Therefore, avoid badly oxygenated surroundings – for example, far inside a shallow, heavily vegetated cove. By contrast, a channel is always oxygen-rich due to constant water circulation.

Among other points to remember for keeping baitfish alive and healthy as long as possible, do not mix large and small bait together. The bigger fish's stronger movements expose the smaller fish to great strain. Neither should one mix perch together with "soft" fish, because of the perch's thorny fins.

Corves for short-time preservation

Keeping baitfish alive between fishing tours can save plenty of work during a long winter. In the short term, of course, it may be tempting after a whole fishing day to throw back unused

A 100-litre herring cask is somewhat clumsy to handle. But both smelt and large roach can spend a long time in such a corf. A butterfly net with a far-reaching arm is appreciated when retrieving live bait from this cupboard.

bait through a hole in the ice, and drive straight home with a little less to haul and deal with. And this is no problem, provided that one is sure of having access to unlimited amounts of bait. Once again, though: how many fishing trips have had to be cancelled because of lack of bait, or because one has lacked enough foresight?

As noted earlier, corfing of baitfish in their natural environment is best. But if necessity leads you to try a type of short-time preservation, such alternatives also exist. Preservation for a short time may mean keeping the fish in a bait-bucket on your balcony, if the temperature outside is not too far below freezing. Let the bucket stand on some insulating base and, if possible, wrap it in something similar. Change the water once or twice daily, and take the bucket inside occasionally for a few hours if ice begins to form in it.

This kind of bait preservation without an air pump is feasible only during the winter, as the water is well-cooled and the fish consume extremely little oxygen in comparison with the summer half-year. Still, one must be careful not to keep too many baits in the same bucket.

Finally, a word about your bathtub. As long as the other members of the household do not object, you might occasionally ask for permission to borrow the bathtub overnight.

The winter's Catch & Release

Ever more sportfishermen find it meaningful to release the fish they catch. But not all know how this should be done in a way that is gentle to the fish. As a result, many fish meet a painful fate, often leading to death after their "release". If there is an ecological or ethical idea behind the releasing of caught fish, the idea is distorted unless the fish are released in a suitable manner.

Damage to the fish's protective layer of slime is common during the catch. Such damage gives rise to "burn injuries", and eventually to infectious and fungal diseases. In warm summer water, bacteria take over rapidly and wreak havoc. In the winter's cold water, the fish have a greater chance of self-healing.

The fish that survive best are those which are quickly and simply unhooked while still in the water. This causes negligible damage to the fish's outer slime layer. Fish that have been hooked farther inside the mouth face bigger dangers – especially if the fisherman lacks suitable tools to release the fish rapidly with. In such a case, if you also place the fish on dry land or frozen snow, where it tumbles around while the difficult operation of freeing it is performed, the effect on the fish can be disastrous.

With proper disgorging tools (see the illustration!) and with careful handling in general, however, the fish need not suffer damage from being freed. Part of the cautious handling may be, if necessary, that the fish is held with wet hands, or placed on a wet smooth base, while the hooks are loosened. As a rule, the more quickly and deftly the operation is performed, the better the fish feels.

Bleeding can also be a cause of incorrect releasing. Small bleeding often seems to stop by itself after a short time, and appears not to harm the fish seriously. Moreover, fish are evidently tolerant of external bloodshed on the body. On the other hand, damage in the mouth may be another matter. A seriously injured or torn-off gill can produce so much bleeding that the fish is doomed to die at the same moment it is released.

A pike being released through the ice hole.

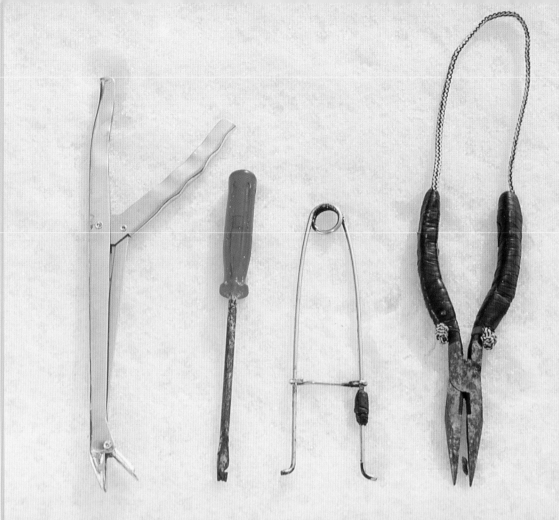

If the fishing is conducted by the catch-and-release method, this measure should be carried out as fast and gently as possible, which is possible only if the fisherman has access to suitable disgorging tools.

Below:
Even a messy situation is soon resolved when the right equipment is at hand.

Even injury to the soft palate – the thin flap of skin that protects the fish's palate down to the throat – can cause strong bleeding if any central blood vessel is damaged. Fish with this type of bleeding should be kept for awhile under observation in a so-called carp sack or the like. Then you can soon see whether the bleeding stops and whether the fish is otherwise in such good condition that it can be released with a good conscience. If this possibility does not exist, the fish should not be set back.

Watch out for freeze injuries and eye damage to the fish

Although fish that are released in cold water tend to fare better than those which are set back in warmer waters, winter does bring certain complications.

In catch-and-release winter fishing, a serious risk arises: freeze injuries. There is research to show that a fish's slime layer suffers harm already when the air temperature falls below 4°C (40°F). This can be worth remembering, especially if the wind is blowing at the same time. Not much wind is needed to turn a temperature slightly above freezing to one that is well below.

Consequently, the slime layer of a fish is very sensitive to freeze injuries. And so are its eyes! When exposed to freezing temperatures, the eyes soon become grey and dull. Even before the cornea begins to acquire this colour, the damage process is under way. When releasing fish in the winter, it is thus extremely important to keep this in mind. Place either yourself or the fish at an angle that protects it from the wind!

Best of all is to free the fish quickly from the hook while it is still in the water-filled ice hole. But placing the fish in a wet plastic bag can also provide good protection for both the eyes and body during the disgorging.

In sum: catch-and-release is not a haphazard action – it is an attitude that the fisherman has decided upon and prepared before the fishing tour.

Index

Index